Vegetable by Vegetable
A Guide for Gardening Near the Salish Sea

Marko Colby & Hanako Myers
Illustrated by Hanako Myers

Published by Midori Farm LLC

ISBN: 978-0-578-10480-5

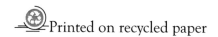Printed on recycled paper

Printed in the USA by Instantpublisher.com

Contents

The Salish Sea

The Salish Sea is the name recently adopted by the people and governments of Washington State and British Columbia for the inland sea encompassing the Puget Sound, Hood Canal, the Strait of Juan de Fuca, the Strait of Georgia and Desolation Sound and all of the adjoining waterways. While each of these bodies of water is unique in its own way, together they form a single marine ecosystem not bound by artificial borders. The influence of this marine ecosystem on the surrounding land is so great that it (along with the surrounding mountains) shapes and defines this ground on which we live and garden.

The consistently moderate water temperatures of the Salish Sea regulate the air temperatures of the nearby land, making summer temperatures cooler and winter temperatures warmer than areas even slightly more inland. The moderating effect of the sea unites all gardeners who plant near her shores. The growing season on Vashon Island, Washington has much more in common with that of Campbell River, BC, 220 miles (350 kilometers) to the north than it does with the growing season in Cle Elum, Washington just 80 miles (120 kilometers) to the east.

The Salish Sea
& Surrounding Basin
The Salish Sea extends from the north end of the Strait
of Georgia to the south end of the Puget Sound and
west to the mouth of the Strait of Juan de Fuca

Map of the Salish Sea & Surrounding Basin, Stefan Freelan, WWU, 2009

Introduction

Vegetable gardening is one of the most sublime pleasures. There is a deep satisfaction that comes from working the soil, tending to plants and creating our meals from start to finish. Gardening taps into our primal need to provide for ourselves and our families, to gather, to be outdoors in all kinds of weather, to observe the natural world and to witness its power and magic.

Here in the Maritime Northwest, the large bodies of seawater nearby greatly influence our weather and create unique challenges and opportunities for the vegetable grower. In our often cool summers, the effort to ripen flavorful heat-loving crops such as tomatoes and peppers can be a lifelong quest. However, the temperature moderating effect of the sea often makes for a long growing season that allows for a year-round harvest of many other vegetables.

This guide grew out of our experience as organic market gardeners living near Port Townsend, Washington, which is arguably one of the kookiest growing climates in our region. Frigid winds in July are common, as are early and late hard freezes and even warm winters where the cilantro just won't die. We grow 4 acres of organic vegetables and operate a vegetable seedling business growing over 100,000 seedlings a year for sale to local gardeners. During our time selling plants we have noticed that many gardeners have very basic questions about how to care for their seedlings: how to plant, water, feed and harvest. There are numerous books written on the topic of Northwest gardening and our mission is not to duplicate material that already exists, but to share what we have learned with the aim of giving straightforward answers to those broad questions our customers ask us each season.

The bulk of the information in this guide will apply to gardens anywhere within a day's walk of the Salish Sea. There are, of course, numerous micro-climates within this region and all of the planting information should be adjusted accordingly.

Gardening information is personal and circumstantial...what has worked for us may not work for other gardeners. We have attempted to gather our experiences, what has and has not worked for us, into a guide that will help novice gardeners get started and hopefully provide some insight for more experienced growers as well.

Happy Gardening!

Marko Colby & Hanako Myers

Seeds:
Organic, Open-pollinated, Hybrid, Heirloom and GMO

Seeds are tiny plants enclosed in protective coating along with a bit of stored food. They are fertilized (pollinated) plant egg cells that have begun to grow at the moment of pollination (while on the mother plant), then gone dormant once the embryonic plant is fully encapsulated. The seed then waits until conditions are perfect to resume growth, this is when germination occurs. Once the right combination of variables is present (temperature and moisture being the two most important), the seed breaks its dormancy and begins to unfurl into what we call a plant.

Seeds are endlessly fascinating; they are the starting and ending point of any vegetable garden. Seeds can be large and very durable, such as a coconut, or so fine that they can be transported great distances by wind and birds or other animals. Some seeds can withstand fire and digestion by animals (or even require it for germination). Some seeds can remain dormant for hundreds of years, just waiting until the conditions are perfect for germination. Every parent plant starts out as a seed itself, and given the opportunity will go through the processes of sexual reproduction: germination, growth, maturation, flowering, pollination and seed formation. The seeds we plant are the final product of this process, they are the offspring, and with them the cycle continues.

The most important thing to know is that the best seeds to plant are those that come from a healthy strain of plants that are well-suited for growing in the specific conditions of your area. The best way to be sure of this is to purchase seeds from a good source, preferably a reputable local or regional seed company, or to grow your own seeds from healthy and productive plants. Talk to other gardeners in your area to find out what varieties have performed well for them and where they procured their seeds. Tomatoes are a particularly good example of the importance of choosing varieties wisely. There are thousands of unique varieties of tomatoes from all around the world. However, there may only be thirty or so that will mature well in an outdoor garden in the cool summers common around the Salish Sea. An early-maturing tomato in Central Oregon is a late-maturing tomato in most gardens around the Salish Sea. There are varieties of tomatoes that are grown and have been maintained in this region for many successive seasons by astute seed savers collecting seed from only those plants that mature early and that show resistance to common regional diseases. This is how locally adapted varieties or strains of vegetables come to exist and these are the ones that are important to learn about and appropriate to plant.

Organic seeds are important for the organic gardener because they have been bred for and grown under organic conditions. Organic gardens often have more weeds, more disease and more damaging insects present than non-organic gardens. Seeds bred and selected in organic conditions will be much more likely to grow well in an organic garden than seeds bred in the sterile conditions of a non-organic garden.

Seed Terminology

Open pollinated (OP) seed, both organic and non-organic, comes from plants allowed to freely self-pollinate or cross-pollinate with other plants of the same species. Gardeners and farmers have selected plants this way for thousands of years, aiming to collect seed from the strongest plants or the plants that have shown unique or desirable characteristics. This technique allows gardeners and farmers to select for traits that are regionally specific and which are adaptable over time to changing conditions. There are many great open-pollinated varieties available commercially. Unfortunately, there has been minimal effort in the commercial realm towards creating stronger and better adapted open-pollinated varieties and thus many are in need of improvement.

Seed from open-pollinated varieties may be grown and saved by the home gardener, though with certain species, saving seed from too small of a population may result in weakening of the genes due to inbreeding depression. This occurs when there is not enough genetic variability.

Heirloom seed is saved from open-pollinated plant varieties that have stabilized and been maintained for a long period of time, often from generation to generation and often from a single family or geographic region. Just how old a variety needs to be to be considered an heirloom is a subject of much debate. Opinions range from thirty to one hundred years old. Heirloom seed may be organic or non-organic. Heirlooms often have some unique characteristic (taste, color, etc.) that makes them popular though they are not always the strongest growing, most disease resistant or most delicious varieties available.

Hybrid seed is produced by crossing two distinct varieties of the same species that each have proven and consistent desirable traits such as uniformity, disease resistance, or yield. When the two varieties are crossed the combining of genetic information creates a stronger, more vigorous plant than either of the parent strains were on their own. In order to produce that same hybrid variety each season, the two parent lines must be maintained separately and they must be kept free from any cross-contamination (pollination by other plants of the same species). Hybridization is a human controlled natural process that has been a part of classical plant breeding since the early 1900's. Hybrid seed is not genetically modified. Due to the complexity of this process, hybrid seed is usually produced by larger seed companies with vested economic interests. Seed saved from hybrid plants usually does not produce "true-to-type" (this means it does not exhibit traits that are the same as its parents and to the rest of the plants in its generation) and thus is not usually saved by the home gardener who desires consistency. Hybrid seed is available as organic and non-organic.

GMO (Genetically Modified Organism) seed comes from plants whose genetic makeup has been altered by recombinant DNA technology. This technology allows genetic material to be combined in a way that could not naturally occur. This process can only be performed in a laboratory setting. This seed is available commercially, though not many home garden seed companies sell GMO seed. The debate about GMO seed is complex and we will not deeply broach the subject here. From an organic home gardener's or farmer's perspective, GMO seed can be dangerous as its impact on the natural world is not yet fully understood. Also, its altered genetic information can contaminate organic seed crops if both are produced in close enough proximity. If you do not wish to use GMO seed, be certain to get seed from sources that claim their seed is GMO-free. If you are concerned about GMO issues your best bet is to always purchase organic seed from a reputable company or grow your own seed. See our resources section for more information.

Starting Seeds

A garden begins with three ingredients: soil, seed and water. Gardeners can learn to start their own seeds by following a few basic guidelines. The general rule of thumb is to plant a seed three times as deep as its width into a loose fertile soil. Think of a seed as an energy packet for the emerging plant. A very light, small seed has less energy to get the seedling through the crust of the soil and up into light, so it needs to be planted at a shallow depth. A large seed has more storage of energy, so it can emerge from deeper in the soil and should therefore be planted deeper. It is advantageous to plant a seed as deep in the soil as the seed will allow because there will be more consistent moisture down there and this allows the gardener to water less frequently. The top quarter inch of soil can dry out rapidly and this requires constant monitoring to make sure that the soil remains moist during germination of small, shallow-planted seeds.

Direct seeding is when the seed is planted directly into the garden soil. This is the best method for vegetables that do not like to have their roots disturbed, including most root vegetables such as carrots and parsnips, and bulbing stem vegetables such as radishes and turnips. Direct seeding has its advantages: there is no transplant shock, the seedling can grow undisturbed once it has emerged, it eliminates one step for the gardener, it requires no special equipment or tools. There are disadvantages as well: the gardener has less control over the environment in which the tender seedlings are growing, as a result there can be more problems with temperature, soil moisture, insects and weeds. In addition, there is less opportunity to select which plants make it into the garden based on their health, size and vigor.

Tips for Direct Seeding

- ⅄ Start with a fertile, deeply worked soil that is free of weeds.
- ⅄ Plant seeds to the correct depth. Most seed packets will provide the specifics of this.
- ⅄ Keep the soil evenly moist, but not waterlogged, until the seed has germinated. Once the seeds have germinated, regular, deep watering is more appropriate.
- ⅄ Plant seeds at the appropriate time. Wait until air and soil temperatures have warmed up before planting heat-loving vegetables. It does no good to rush the process.
- ⅄ Protect germinating seeds from damaging pests.

Seeding for transplanting is when a seed is sown into a soil mix in a pot or other container (in a greenhouse, cold frame, sunny south-facing window or outdoors if later in the season). When the plant is of appropriate size it is planted out into the garden. There are many advantages of transplanting. The plant is bigger and hardier when it is planted into the garden, thus it has a better chance at surviving insect damage, weed pressure and variable temperatures and weather conditions. Starting seeds in pots also gives the gardener more control over the growing environment (water, air temperature, soil temperature and potential insect damage) during seed germination. The disadvantages are that this requires some amount of special equipment (soil, pots, etc.) and requires space to perform the work and grow the seedlings (window sill, cold frame or greenhouse).

Tips for Starting Seeds for Transplanting

- ⅄ Use a good quality organic potting mix either purchased or your own mix made from a combination of garden soil, peat moss and finished compost. A sterile potting mix can be beneficial for some sensitive seeds.
- ⅄ Water germinating seeds enough to keep soil moist but not waterlogged. Too much water is a common problem, leading to death of seedlings from damping-off fungi.

- Provide airflow around the plants: fans, natural wind, etc.
- Ensure a natural night and day light cycle. Avoid too much or too little light exposure.
- Allow for a gentle transition from a controlled environment to the real world of the garden, this is called "hardening off" the plants. Introduce the plant gradually to the outside word, a little bit more each day for a few days, then keep it outside in its pot for a couple of days and nights in a protected spot before planting into the garden.
- Keep heat-loving crops from freezing or from spending too much time in cool, wet soils.

Soil Fertility in the Salish Garden

Fertility in the garden can be as simple or as complex as the gardener wishes it to be. A good garden soil will have the ability to hold water, nutrient and air. A loose, crumbly texture to a depth of at least 8 inches is ideal. Good drainage is essential. Most garden plants do not grow well if their roots are sitting in water.

To keep a garden soil healthy without putting too much thought into the process, simply spread a couple of inches of well-aged compost onto the garden each year and work it in with a digging fork, shovel or rake. Most soils will also benefit from the addition of a well-balanced organic fertilizer blend each season. Vegetables that require extra nutrition can be side dressed with compost or fertilizer again mid-season. Gardens in this area will be improved 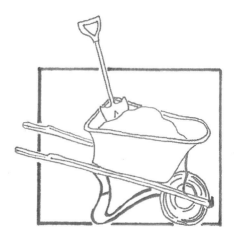 greatly by the addition of a bit of agricultural lime every other year. This provides much needed calcium to the plants and also helps to make the soil less acidic.

Annual vegetables are heavy feeders. This means that a gardener will need to add materials to the soil every year to keep it well fed. If you feed the soil, the soil will in turn feed the vegetables. This process is called mineralization. Garden soil is like a pet. It needs to be fed and watered and in return it will provide unconditional love and the plants will thrive. Garden soil is actually a symbiotic collection of visible and invisible beings made up of earthworms, micro-organisms, fungi, bacteria, nematodes and other non-living ingredients. A single teaspoon of healthy soil contains up to one billion bacteria and several yards of fungal hyphae! The millions of creatures that live in garden soil work to break down organic materials in the soil, such as manure, rocks and plant materials and to turn them into something that growing plants can use. This process takes energy. To fuel that energy intensive process the soil needs food. We feed the soil any time we add compost or other organic materials such as rock powders, dry fertilizers, grass clippings or cover crops.

Compost is an essential component to a healthy garden. Good compost supplies macro-nutrients such as nitrogen, phosphorus, potassium, magnesium, sulfur and some micro-nutrients as well. It also feeds the soil food web by adding organic matter to the soil along with beneficial bacteria and fungi. Well-finished compost should smell pleasant and feel light and fluffy. If it smells rotten or is otherwise disgusting, it is not yet composted and should not be used on the garden. Compost can be made at home or purchased from a reputable garden store or local farmer. Well-aged manure (at least a couple of years old) may be substituted for compost though often times it will contain a high quantity of weed seeds. Never use fresh manure on a vegetable garden as it may contain pathogenic bacteria and will also contain too much nitrogen which can damage young plants.

Garden soil around the Salish Sea varies greatly from site to site. Because all garden soils start off with different levels of nutrients, just adding good compost to a new garden site may not be enough to grow healthy plants. Sending garden soil to a professional for testing is a worthwhile investment. (See resources section at the end of book for soil test resources.) A soil test will give the gardener some baseline data concerning which macro-nutrients and micro-nutrients the soil is lacking or has in excess, the pH level of the soil and usually a few other details. Most professional soil tests will make recommendations on how much of which specific nutrient to add to the garden in order to balance the soil.

Vegetable by Vegetable

The vegetables in this guide are grouped together by family. Vegetables within the same family often have similar growing requirements and it is important for the gardener to recognize the families in order to practice good crop rotation. Garden plants are often referred to first by the family name, then the genus and then the species. For example: cabbage is in the family Brassicaceae, the genus *Brassica* and the species is *oleracea*.

Taxonomy, the science of naming and classifying plants is an ever-changing field of study. With the recent advent of genetic mapping many plants have been reclassified and/or renamed. We imagine this trend will continue, therefore, please forgive us if any of our names are currently incorrect or become incorrect in the future.

Amaranthaceae Family

Beet (*Beta vulgaris*)

General Comments: Beets come in all sorts of colors and shapes. They can be grown for the roots, the greens or both. Regardless of what variety is chosen a beet is a rewarding and easy vegetable to grow. Occasionally beets planted too early or exposed to prolonged cold spells in the early season will go to seed prematurely due to false vernalization. Cover beets sown earlier than late-March with row cover or a cloche.
Seeding Depth: ½ inch.
Seeding for Transplant: Early March through late June. Beets can be transplanted, but direct seeding is recommended.
Direct Seeding: Late March to early July.

12

Plant Spacing: Thin to 2-6 inches apart in all directions. More space between plants encourages larger beets. Because each seed is actually a cluster of seeds, beets emerge densely and require thinning if being grown for the root.

Soil/Fertility: Needs moderate to high fertility, a well-balanced soil with plenty of organic matter will grow the best beets.

Water: Consistent moisture grows the most tender roots.

Harvest: For greens: any time. For roots: any time after the beets begin to form bulbs. Young beets are incredibly tender. Older, very large beets may start to get woody in texture.

Pests: Leaf miner can bore holes into leaves and lay eggs, usually damage is only done to some leaves and will not impact the entire plant. Destroy impacted leaves.

Disease: Mostly disease-free, though a fungus that forms scabs can form on the roots. Damage is purely aesthetic. To control scab, practice a good crop rotation and avoid using fresh manure or unfinished compost.

Winter Harvest: Suitable for winter harvest. If mulched heavily with straw, beets can last the entire winter in the garden, though rot at the crown is common.

Swiss chard (*Beta vulgaris*)

General Comments: Chard is the same plant as beet but has been selected over time for its tender leaves and not for its root. It is a beautiful and delicious plant that can last an entire season in the garden if picked lightly. For a continued, frequent harvest plant chard two or three times during the growing season.

Seeding Depth: ½ inch.

Seeding for Transplant: Early March to mid-July.

13

Direct Seeding: Late March to early July.

Plant Spacing: 4-12 inches in all directions. More space between plants encourages larger plants and leaves.

Soil/Fertility: Needs fertile, well-balanced soil with plenty of organic matter.

Water: Consistent moisture produces the most tender leaves, though we have seen chard volunteer in a non-irrigated part of the garden and thrive.

Harvest: Can be picked any time by cutting or snapping off the stems of the larger leaves at the base of the plant, letting the smaller, central leaves grow. May be grown at closer spacing and harvested for baby-sized leaves.

Pests: Leaf miner can bore holes into leaves and lay eggs, usually damage is done only to some leaves and will not impact the entire plant. Destroy impacted leaves.

Disease: Can be affected by powdery mildew.

Winter Harvest: Chard leaves will die in a hard freeze, though often the plant will survive and grow new leaf material when temperatures rise. White chard seems to be the most winter hardy of chards.

Spinach (*Spinacea oleracea*)

General Comments: Spinach is a fairly easy crop to grow. Highest quality harvests come from early spring and late summer plantings when the days are shorter and temperatures are a bit cooler. Late spring and early summer plantings have a tendency to bolt quickly, so pick promptly.

Seeding Depth: ¼ to ½ inch.

Seeding for Transplant: March through April.

Direct Seeding: Direct seeding is recommended. Late March to early September. Mid-August/early September is the ideal planting time for late fall harvests.

Plant Spacing: For full sized leaves: 4-6 inches apart in all directions. For baby cutting leaf: 40 seeds per foot.

Soil/Fertility: Needs moderate fertility and a well-drained soil.

Water: Needs consistent moisture, do not overwater.

Harvest: For baby-leaf: cut the entire plant for re-growth. For larger leaves: harvest outer leaves, allowing the inner leaves to continue growing.

Pests: Mostly insect-free.

Disease: Mostly disease-free, though susceptible to some viral infections and downy mildew. Destroy infected plants.

Winter Harvest: Some varieties will overwinter, especially with the use of row cover or cloche.

Amaryllidaceae Family

Onion, Shallot (*Allium cepa*)

General Comments: Onions from seed are generally healthier and less likely to bolt than those grown from sets. (If you do not wish to start your own onions early in the season, purchasing onion plants is a good option. For this latitude be sure to choose long-day varieties for good bulb formation. Many modern varieties of shallots may also be grown from seed following the same technique as for onions. Shallots not grown from seed are grown like garlic. Scallions are simply "regular" onions that tend not to make bulbs and are usually planted very close together and harvested young.

Seeding Depth: ¼ inch.

Seeding for Transplant: For long-day bulbing onions and shallots: January through February. Spanish sweets (walla walla type) may also be sown in July and transplanted in September to overwinter and harvest in early June. For scallions or green onions: January through August.

Direct Seeding: As early as possible. Bulbing onions: mid-April at the latest. Scallions: may be sown through June for fall harvest and throughout August for overwintering and harvesting in the spring.

Plant Spacing: Bulbing onions and shallots: 4-6 inches apart in all directions. Cippolini and mini onions: 2-3 inches apart in all directions. Scallions: ¼ to ½" apart, do not require thinning.

Soil/Fertility: Needs moderate to high fertility with plenty of organic matter. Most alliums benefit from plenty of available calcium.

Water: Consistent watering is crucial, especially during bulb formation.

Harvest: May be harvested and eaten at any stage of growth. When the plants finish their life cycle the tops will fall over, signaling the end of the growth cycle and thus the time to pull the mature onion or shallot out of the ground. To cure onions and shallots, place the bulbs with the greens still attached in a warm, dry, shaded place that has ample air flow (fans are helpful) for 2 to 3 weeks. When the tops have dried, cut them off, brush off dirt and cut off the roots and place bulbs in storage in a dry place at room temperature.

Pests: Mostly insect-free.

Disease: Rusts, rots, and many fungal diseases are common. Good garden sanitation is key as is maintaining a good rotation. A minimum five year rotation between all allium crops is highly recommended.

Winter Harvest: Bulb onions are not suitable for winter harvest. Some scallions are hardy enough for winter harvest.

Leek (*Allium porrum*)

General Comments: Leeks are generally grown similarly to onions. They can be eaten at baby size or full size. For overwintering leeks be sure to select a variety that is very cold hardy.
Seeding Depth: ¼ inch.
Seeding for Transplant: For full-sized fall/winter leeks: early February through April. For overwintered leeks to be harvested in the early spring: May through June.
Direct Seeding: As early as the soil can be worked through mid-July.
Plant Spacing: 4-6 inches between plants in all directions. It is nice to plant them in rows allowing for hilling of the growing plant, this encourages longer shafts.
Soil/Fertility: Needs moderate fertility. Benefits from available calcium.
Water: Consistent. Avoid letting the soil completely dry out.
Harvest: Any time, though best in the late fall, winter and early spring.

Pests: Mostly insect-free.
Disease: Rusts, rots and many fungal diseases are common. Good garden sanitation is key as is maintaining a good rotation. A minimum five year rotation between all allium crops is highly recommended.
Winter Harvest: Great for winter harvest. Make sure to plant a very cold-hardy variety.

Garlic (*Allium sativum*)

General Comments: Garlic is usually grown by planting healthy, disease-free cloves of garlic. Each clove planted will yield a full head. Plant the hard root end down and the pointy end up. Many growers prefer to mulch their garlic at time of planting. This protects the garlic from hard freezes in the winter, prevents weed growth and eliminates or reduces the need for watering. In early summer some garlic sends up long hard stems from their centers which will produce flowers and seed heads called scapes. Just as the flower bud begins to swell it is necessary to remove the scape by snapping or cutting the stalk where it comes out of the top sets of leaves. This stops the process of seed formation and redirects the energies of the plant toward the bulb, increasing its size. The scapes are a culinary treat and may be used similarly to garlic.

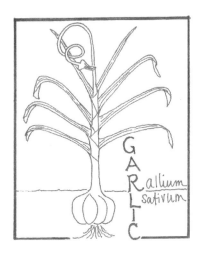

Softneck and Hardneck Types: There are two main types of garlic, hardneck and softneck. This refers to the stem or neck of the plant. Softneck garlic is a stemless garlic that usually produces a large quantity of small cloves. Softneck varieties tend to have better storage capabilities, often keeping until spring. Hardneck garlic has firm stems and can make flower heads (scapes). Hardneck varieties tend to produce fewer and larger cloves per head and do not usually keep much past the new year. Some garlic aficionados claim that hardneck garlic has the most complex flavors.

Seeding Depth: 2 inches.
Seeding for Transplant: Does not transplant well, not recommended.
Direct Seeding: Break heads apart into cloves and plant whole

cloves any time from mid-September to mid-November. Softneck varieties may even be planted in early spring with moderate success.

Plant Spacing: 4-6 inches apart in all directions. The more space given, the larger the heads will grow.

Soil/Fertility: Needs moderate to high fertility and good drainage. Fertilize with compost when planting in the fall and for the largest bulbs, side-dress in the spring with more compost or other well-balanced fertilizer.

Water: If garlic is mulched, it may not need any water at all during the growing season. If it is not mulched, keep the soil moist until early June, then stop watering altogether. Let the soil completely dry out before harvest begins in July. Be careful not to overwater as this can lead to fungal and mold issues.

Harvest: Dig garlic when the leaves of the plant begin to dry from the bottom of the plant towards the top, this will generally be in late summer. It is best to harvest when approximately half of the leaves have dried and the other half remain green. Each leaf represents a layer of wrapper on the bulb. If harvested when all the leaves are green, there will be too much moisture in the wrappers and this will stymie the curing process. If harvested after all the leaves have dried, there is a good chance that the wrappers will not remain on the bulb to protect the cloves on the inside, thus decreasing the length of storage life. Brush dirt off the roots, but leave the roots on. Bring the garlic into a shady, dry and well-ventilated area to finish drying. This is the curing process, which allows garlic to keep well into the winter. Store at room temperature in a dry and dark location.

Pests: Mostly insect-free.

Disease: Rusts, rots and fungal diseases are common. Proper garden sanitation is crucial, as is good crop rotation. A minimum of five years in between allium family crops is recommended. If there is garlic rot present, discontinue growing all allium family crops (garlic in particular) for a minimum of seven years.

Winter Harvest: Not recommended.

Apiaceae Family

Carrot (*Daucus carota*)

General Comments: There are many varieties of carrots. There are fat crunchy chantenay types that grow well in heavy soils, sugary sweet nantes types that love a deep sandy soil, carrots the color of the rainbow and even little round Parisian carrots the size and shape of a golf ball. In general any well-worked soil free of rocks will produce good carrots.

Seeding Depth: ¼ inch.

Seeding for Transplant: Does not transplant well, not recommended.

Direct Seeding: March through July.

Plant Spacing: Seed heavily and thin to 1-2 inches apart with rows 8-24 inches apart or thin to 2 inches apart in all directions for block planting.

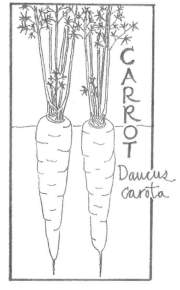

Soil/Fertility: Carrots like a loose soil worked to a depth of about 10". Avoid too much nitrogen as this will cause hairy roots and splitting. (We usually do not fertilize our carrot beds.)

Water: Water deeply on a weekly basis or as needed. Too much water will grow soft carrots.

Harvest: Any time, though the most flavorful carrots are usually harvested after 2 months once they have begun to size up and develop good color.

Pests: Carrot rust fly lays eggs at the base of the plants and the young maggots burrow into and feed on the roots. Use floating row cover at time of seeding for pest exclusion. Early season plantings of carrots can usually escape rust fly damage if harvested young.

Disease: The foliage can be susceptible to some fungal disease, choose disease resistant varieties if this is a problem.
Winter Harvest: A great crop for harvest through the winter. Sow seeds by mid-July and mulch with straw before the first hard freeze arrives.

Parsnip (*Pastinaca sativa*)

General Comments: Culture is similar to carrots, though parsnips usually take over 100 days to fully mature. They are best grown for harvest late in the year after frosts have increased the sweetness.
Seeding Depth: ¼ to ½ inch.
Seeding for Transplant: Does not transplant well, not recommended.
Direct Seeding: Throughout May. Parsnips are very slow to germinate (up to 3 weeks) and slow to grow to maturity.
Plant Spacing: Sow seeds heavily and thin to 3-6 inches between plants.
Soil/Fertility: Avoid too much nitrogen as this will cause hairy roots and splitting. Parsnips like a loose soil worked to a depth of about 10 inches.

Water: Slow to germinate from seed, keep seed bed continually moist until germination. During the growing season water deeply as needed, avoid overwatering.
Harvest: Harvest as needed any time after the first good frost as this increases sugar content.
Pests: Highly prone to carrot rust fly damage. Cover with row cover at time of seeding and keep covered until harvest.
Disease: Mostly disease-free.
Winter Harvest: One of the hardiest root vegetables, parsnips will overwinter with minimal attention. Mulch with straw in the fall and harvest until spring.

Celery and Celery Root (*Apium graveolens*)

General Comments: Botanically speaking, these are the same plant, just selected for two different traits. Celery is bred for the tender, flavorful stems and celery root, also known as celeriac, is bred for the solid, celery-flavored bulbous roots. They both take some extra effort to grow as they require special attention to soil fertility and soil moisture. Be cautious not to let the plants freeze when they are in the seedling stage or be exposed to temperatures below 50 degrees for more than 120 hours as this can lead to premature flowering (bolting).

Seeding Depth: Just barely cover with soil.

Seeding for Transplant: Late March to early June, this is the recommend method.

Direct Seeding: Late April to mid-June, the seed is very slow to germinate so be sure to keep seed bed moist until germination.

Plant Spacing: 8-12 inches apart in all directions.

Soil/Fertility: Needs high fertility with a bit of extra nitrogen. Depending on the existing soil fertility, try adding extra compost and/or dry organic fertilizer blend at planting and then top dressing mid-season.

Water: Wild celery grows in mucky wet soils. Garden celery, as well as celeriac, likes a similarly moist soil. Keep the soil evenly moist the entire season. Moisture stress can cause the plant to become tough and pithy and even to bolt prematurely.

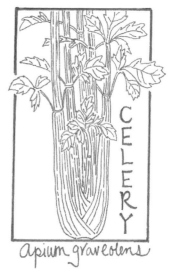

apium graveolens

Harvest: Celery may be harvested any time by cutting the entire head or by breaking off the outer stems as needed. Celery root is usually harvested in the fall by digging the entire root, cutting off the stringy, celery-like stems and washing the root with a powerful spray of water.

Pests: Mostly insect-free, though celery root can occasionally be impacted by carrot rust fly. If this is a problem in your garden you may consider using row cover for pest exclusion.

Disease: Mostly disease-free.

Winter Harvest: Celery can withstand light frosts and still be fine to eat, best if harvested by Thanksgiving time. Celery root will hold in the ground fairly well through the winter if given a heavy straw mulch.

Fennel (*Foeniculum vulgare*)

General Comments: Growing fennel is easy. Growing fennel that produces nice large bulbs is not necessarily so. It will grow anywhere with little attention, but if the goal is to produce a large, tender, sweet bulb of fennel, attention to detail is required. If growing from transplants, be careful to not let the plant become root bound in the pot and minimize root disturbance during planting as both can lead to bolting.

Seeding Depth: ¼ inch.

Seeding for Transplant: For best bulb formation, May through June.

Direct Seeding: May to early July. Recommended method.

Plant Spacing: 6-8 inches apart in all directions.

Soil/Fertility: Needs highly fertile, well-balanced soil with lots of organic matter for consistent bulb formation.

Water: Needs consistent moisture. Do not let the soil completely dry out.

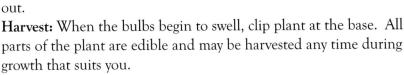

Harvest: When the bulbs begin to swell, clip plant at the base. All parts of the plant are edible and may be harvested any time during growth that suits you.

Pests: Mostly insect-free.

Disease: Mostly disease-free, with occasional fungal disease on the leaves though this rarely impacts quality of harvest.

Winter Harvest: Can tolerate light frosts, but not hard freezes.

Parsley (*Petroselinum crispum*)

General Comments: Parsley is a wonderful culinary herb that can be harvested almost year-round in the Maritime Northwest. A few well-timed sowings throughout the year will provide a continuous supply. Parsley does well in pots. Choose between curly leaf and the more flavorful Italian flat leaf.

Seeding Depth: Just barely cover with soil.

Seeding for Transplant: Early March through July. (Late July sowings will overwinter small and begin re-growth in spring.)

Direct Seeding: April through July.

Plant Spacing: 12 inches in all directions.

Soil/Fertility: Needs moderate fertility. As with most leafy greens, higher fertility translates to increased growth.

Water: Seed is slow to germinate, so be sure to keep moist during this time. Consistent moisture will produce the best tasting leaves and helps reduce chances of premature bolting.

Harvest: Harvest outer leaves by snapping the mature stem at the base of the plant, letting the inner leaves continue to grow.

Pests: Mostly insect-free.

Disease: Mostly disease-free.

Winter Harvest: Will usually overwinter in the garden for continued harvest.

Cilantro and Coriander (*Coriandrum sativum*)

General Comments: Cilantro is a quick-growing culinary herb that can withstand cool soils and light frosts. Cilantro bolts (goes to seed) quickly, so for continued harvest sow new seeds every few weeks. Coriander is the mature seed of any cilantro plant. For mature coriander seed plant early in the season and allow the plant to make seed.

Seeding Depth: ¼ inch.

Seeding for Transplant: Early March through August.
Direct Seeding: Recommended method. Mid-March to early September.
Plant Spacing: Sow thickly in rows 6 inches apart. For coriander seed thin to 6 inches apart between plants.
Soil/Fertility: Will grow almost anywhere, though a moderately fertile soil will produce the most abundant plants.
Water: Consistent moisture will increase leaf growth.
Harvest: Any time during growth. All parts are edible. Will re-grow after cutting.
Pests: Mostly insect-free.
Disease: Mostly disease-free.
Winter Harvest: Can handle light frosts and does well in cold frames or greenhouse during the winter.

Dill (*Antheum graveolens*)

General Comments: An easy-to-grow culinary herb. May be used in leaf stage or allowed to make flowers or mature seeds which are used for pickling.
Seeding Depth: ¼ to ½ inch.
Seeding for Transplant: April through June.
Direct Seeding: April through June.
Plant Spacing: 2-6 inches apart in all directions.
Soil/Fertility: Needs moderate fertility.

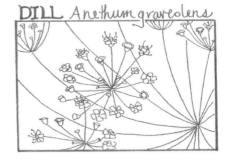

Water: Water as needed to prevent soil from completely drying out.
Harvest: Any time during growth. As the plant matures, leaves may be harvested while allowing the seed head to mature.
Pests: Mostly insect-free.
Disease: Mostly disease-free.
Winter Harvest: Harvest before first frost.

Asteraceae Family

Lettuce (*Lactuca sativa*)

General Comments: Lettuce can be grown from early spring until the first hard freeze for full-sized heads or baby leaf/salad mix. For baby leaf lettuce you may harvest the outer leaves and let the inner leaves grow, or cut the entire plant with a knife and let it re-grow. There is a point at which the re-growth will become tough and bitter, so keep planting successions throughout the growing season. Head lettuce does best with cool consistent temperatures though some types such as Batavian and Green Leaf do well in locations with warmer summers.

Seeding Depth: Just a bit less than ¼ inch.

Seeding for Transplant: Early March to mid-August for full-sized heads. Head lettuce does not hold too long in the garden so for a continued supply, plan for multiple plantings throughout the growing season.

Direct Seeding: April through August. Baby leaf mixes may be direct seeded through mid-September. Direct seeding is the best method for baby leaf salad mix. Seeding salad mix every 2 weeks throughout the growing season is recommended for a continuous harvest.

Plant Spacing: For head lettuce: 12-18 inches in all directions. For salad mix: seed can be sown thickly, roughly 5 seeds per inch, depending on desired harvest size and frequency of harvest.

Soil/Fertility: Needs moderate fertility. Avoid excess nitrogen, needs available soil calcium.

Water: Likes consistent moisture, though too much can cause

26

bottom rot. It is good to let the surface of the soil dry out between waterings. Early morning is the best time to water.

Harvest: Full-sized heads: whenever plant is at ideal size. For butterhead types, waiting until plant has formed a sizable, tight head is recommended. Baby leaf/salad mix: harvest the outer leaves and let the inner leaves grow, or mow all leaves with a knife.

Pests: Slugs. Try capturing or using traps and keep the perimeter of your garden mowed and dry.

Disease: Powdery mildew, downy mildew, bottom rot, other fungal disease. Assure healthy soil by adding compost each season. Crop rotation is important as is ensuring good airflow around the plants.

Note: Tip burn is a common issue with head lettuce in this region. Make sure soil has ample calcium, maintain consistent soil moisture and avoid over-fertilizing. Rapid growth spurts after cool, cloudy weather can cause plants to grow faster than calcium can move up the plant. This is what causes the tips to burn.

Winter Harvest: Lettuce will freeze and turn to mush, but can handle gentle frosts, especially with row cover. Baby lettuce mix will do well in cold frames or greenhouses through the winter.

Endive, Escarole (*Cichorum endiva*), Radicchio (*Cichorum intybus*)

General Comments: In general the chicories are grown similarly to lettuce. They may be grown for a full head or for baby leaf. For best flavor and most reliable head production sow seeds so they will mature in the late summer or fall. Escarole and endive are quicker-growing than radicchio.

Seeding Depth: Just a bit less than ¼ inch.

Seeding for Transplant: Radicchio: early April to mid-July. Endive and escarole: early April to as late as early August depending on variety and days to maturity. For the most reliable heading sow in late June or early July for fall harvest.

Direct Seeding: Full head: early April to early August. Baby leaf: March to early September.

Plant Spacing: Full head: 12 inches in all directions. Baby leaf: 1 inch apart.

Soil/Fertility: Needs only moderate fertility. Avoid too much nitrogen as this can cause tip burn.

Water: Needs consistent moisture, avoid water stress.

Harvest: Any time during growth.

Pests: Generally insect-free.

Disease: Bottom rot is common in some varieties, especially during the late season.

RADICCHIO
Cichorium intybus

Winter Harvest: Chicories are some of the most frost hardy greens that can be grown in our climate (variety dependent). Time planting so that the plants are just maturing in late October, then cover with row cover or grow in a cold frame. Baby leaf chicories are generally hardy and can survive some winters uncovered. When overwintered small, the plants will have good re-growth for late winter and early spring salads. Castlefranco type radicchios are the most frost hardy.

Artichoke *(Cynara spp.)*

General Comments: Artichokes are a tender perennial and a close relative of the common thistle. Most varieties will overwinter in our climate with a little mulch to prevent freezing. They may also be grown as an annual if proper varieties are chosen and if they are started early enough. Some varieties of artichokes may present off-types. These will be recognizable mostly by stunted growth or by off-colors. Discard these and plant only the most vigorous seedlings.

Seeding Depth: ¼ inch.

Seeding for Transplant: January through February. Once seeds have germinated and developed a couple of sets of true leaves, expose plants to 2 weeks of 50 degree temperatures (protect from freezing) to trick the plants into thinking they have gone through a winter (vernalization). This induces fruit production for the first year.

Direct Seeding: Not recommended as there can be numerous off-types that need to be culled before planting.

Plant Spacing: 3 feet in all directions.

Soil/Fertility: Does best in moderately fertile soil. If growing as a perennial, mulch with compost and a complete fertilizer each year.

Water: Prefers a moist soil that has good drainage. Occasional deep watering is best. Be careful not to overwater.

Harvest: Harvest the flower buds just before they begin to open. Each plant should produce several buds that will mature at different times. At the end of the year cut back the plant and mulch.

Pests: Aphids are fairly common, use insecticidal soap as needed.

Disease: Mostly disease-free.

Winter Harvest: Not suitable for winter harvest.

Brassicaceae Family

Broccoli, Cauliflower, Cabbage *(Brassica oleracea)*, Kale *(Brassica oleracea and Brassica napus)*

General Comments: Also known as the cole crops, this family of plants is one of the best loved by gardeners in the Maritime Northwest. All *Brassica oleracea* were selected for specific traits long ago out of the same wild relative. Humans chose to save seed from some plants that formed a head (cabbage) and others that grew tender, sweet leaves (kale). These crops all have a similar culture. They may be direct sown but transplanting is recommended for gaining a head start over weeds and insects.

Seeding Depth: ¼ to ½ inch.
Seeding for Transplant: Early March through July. (Transplant 3-4 weeks after sowing.) Cauliflower does best from mid-summer plantings.
Direct Seeding: Late March through July.
Plant Spacing: 12-18 inches apart in all directions.
Soil/Fertility: Needs high fertility, cauliflower in particular. A nutrient-rich, well-composted soil is best. Calcium availability is important.
Water: Most brassicas have fairly short root systems, therefore they need consistent watering. Avoid letting the soil completely dry out as this may stress the plants and induce bolting (premature seed head formation).
Harvest: Broccoli and cauliflower: once the head has fully formed and before the beads (little flower buds) begin to open. Cabbage: when the head is firm. Kale: may be harvested at any time, picking leaves from the bottom up insures continued growth.
Pests: Cabbage worms and loopers, aphids, root maggot. Use

exclusion techniques such as polyester fabric row cover when the plants are small or use insecticidal soap as needed. Some growers use BT (*Bacillus thuringiensis*) or neem oil to control cabbage worms and loopers.

Disease: Fungal issues are fairly common, so choose disease resistant varieties and provide ample airflow around the plants. Club root can become a problem if proper crop rotation is not practiced. Allow at least a 4 year rotation between all brassica family crops.

Winter Harvest: The heading brassicas will do well until the first really hard freeze. Purple sprouting broccoli and some varieties of overwintering cauliflower may be started in July to overwinter and will make heads in the late winter or early spring.

Rutabaga (*Brassica napus*)

General Comments: May be grown any time of the growing season, though rutabaga does best as a late fall/winter crop. Similar in culture to all other brassica family crops.

Seeding Depth: ¼ to ½ inch.

Seeding for Transplant: Does not transplant well.

Direct Seeding: Late May through June.

Plant Spacing: 6-8 inches in all directions.

Soil/Fertility: Needs moderate fertility. The most tender roots will form in deeply worked and well-composted, fertile soil.

Water: Rutabagas have a shallow root system so be careful not to let the soil completely dry out. Consistent irrigation is important for high quality roots.

Harvest: Any time after the first frosts. (The frost develops the plant's sugars and sweetens it up.)

Pests: Cabbage root maggot is the most problematic pest. Cover with row cover to exclude pests for the entirety of the growing season.

Disease: Mostly disease-free. Fungal disease can occasionally impact leaves though this usually does not impact the roots very much.

Winter Harvest: A great late fall crop and winter crop. Rutabaga may be left in the garden all winter and be harvested as needed. In extra cold areas mulching with straw may be helpful.

Brussels Sprouts (*Brassica oleracea*)

General Comments: A lovely crop to grow for late season harvest. The key to growing good Brussels sprouts is the timing. Ideally your plant will begin making sprouts on the stalk as the weather begins to shift from summer to fall. Therefore, do not start them too early. If started too early the sprouts will not be tight and aphids can be more of a problem.

Seeding Depth: ¼ to ½ inch.

Seeding for Transplant: Early to late May depending on the variety. For varieties that take 110 days or more to mature, start by mid-May and transplant out four weeks later. For earlier maturing varieties, count the number of days to maturity backwards from October 15th. This will be your transplant day. Plan to seed four weeks before this day.

Direct Seeding: May to early June, depending on days to maturity.

Plant Spacing: 18 inches apart in all directions.

Soil/Fertility: Needs high fertility because the plant is in the ground a long time. Excessive nitrogen, however, can attract aphids. If the plant is looking deficient, try top dressing mid-season with compost or a well-balanced fertilizer.

Water: Brussels sprouts have a shallow root system, be careful not to let the soil completely dry out. Consistent irrigation is essential.

Harvest: Once the sprouts have matured and after the first light frosts (this is usually late October). To encourage all of the sprouts on the stalk to mature at close to the same time cut off the apical (top) bud on the plant when the sprouts begin forming. This is generally in mid-September.

Pests: Cabbage worms and loopers, cabbage root maggot and aphids. Be extra vigilant with aphids. If needed, neem oil may be sprayed as sprout buds begin to form. If aphids are a problem, they must be dealt with before the sprouts are mature, otherwise they will infest the sprouts. Interplanting certain flowering plants can be successfully used for aphid control. Alyssum and phacelia are two that attract the predatory wasps and hover flies whose larvae feed on aphids.

Disease: Fungal issues can impact the leaves, allow for plenty of room for airflow around each plant. Club root can become a problem if proper crop rotation is not practiced, allow at least a 4 year rotation between all brassica family crops.

Winter Harvest: A great late fall and winter crop. Some varieties are extra-hardy and can be left in the garden through the winter.

Asian greens, Mustards, Napa Cabbage, Pac Choi, (*Brassica juncea, Brassica rapa*), Arugula (*Eruca sativa*)

General Comments: Culture of these crops is similar to the cole crops above, though they are more sensitive to premature bolting caused by exposure to early season cold and increasing day length in spring, so harvest spring planted crops when they are still small. If growing Napa cabbage in the spring, plant bolt-resistant varieties. When sown in late summer for fall harvest, they hold well in the garden late into the season.

Seeding Depth: ¼ to ½ inch.

Seeding for Transplant: Mid-March to early September.

(Transplanting is not recommended for turnips.) Heading Napa cabbage should be sown by early August.

Direct Seeding: Mid-March to mid-September.

Plant Spacing: For fully headed Napa cabbage plants: 12-18 inches in all directions. For turnips and baby greens: 1-2 inches apart in all directions. If bigger plants are desired allow for more growing space.

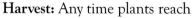

Soil/Fertility: Needs moderate fertility. A well-composted soil is usually enough.

Water: These crops have a shallow root system so they need consistent moisture.

Harvest: Any time plants reach desired size, from small to large, though Napa cabbage is best if allowed to make a firm head before harvesting.

Pests: Cabbage root maggot, cabbage moth, flea beetle, aphids. Use row cover for pest exclusion.

Disease: Susceptible to some fungal and viral disease. Allow for plenty of airflow around varieties that have problems.

Winter Harvest: These are great crops for late fall or winter harvest in cold frames. Can withstand light frosts, however they will freeze to death in a long hard freeze.

Radish including **Daikon,** (*Raphanus sativus*) **Asian Turnip** (*Brassica rapa*)

General Comments: Radishes and Asian turnips are two of the earliest vegetables to plant and harvest as both germinate in very cool soil and grow rapidly. Radishes are best when eaten small before they become overly spicy and pithy. Daikon does best when planted after the summer solstice. Asian turnips are more tender and mild than American turnips. They often called salad turnips. The most mild turnips and radishes are grown during cool temperatures of spring and autumn.

Seeding Depth: ½ inch for radish, ¼ inch for Asian turnips.
Seeding for Transplant: Does not transplant well, not recommended.
Direct Seeding: Early March to mid-September, with the exception of Daikon radish which has a tendency to bolt if planted before the Summer Solstice.
Plant Spacing: For small radishes and turnips:1-2inches in all directions. For large daikon: at least 4 inches apart.
Soil/Fertility: Needs moderate fertility.
Water: Needs consistent moisture to remain tender.

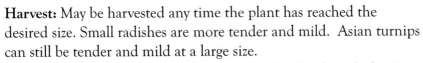

Harvest: May be harvested any time the plant has reached the desired size. Small radishes are more tender and mild. Asian turnips can still be tender and mild at a large size.
Pests: Cabbage root maggot, cabbage moth, flea beetle, aphids. Use row cover for pest exclusion.
Disease: Susceptible to some fungal and viral disease, but it is rare.
Winter Harvest: Great crops for late fall harvest or winter harvest in cold frames. In a long, hard freeze they will freeze to death.

Cucurbitaceae Family

Cucumber *(Cucumis sativus)*, Melon *(Cucumis Melo)* Summer squash, Zucchini *(Cucurbita pepo)*

General Comments: These vegetables are closely related and usually grown under the same conditions. They come in both bushing and vining varieties and this choice will impact your final spacing. They like warm soil, so there is no benefit to starting them early in the season. All cucurbits are prone to damping off in the seedling stage in cool, moist soil, so make sure the soil is warm and irrigate only enough to ensure germination. Early plantings will benefit greatly from protection of row cover or a cloche. Cucumbers may be trained to grow up a trellis, this encourages straighter fruit, especially in long fruited varieties such as the English and Asian types. If growing from transplants it is important to minimize plant stress: try not to let the plants become root bound in their pots and disturb the roots as little as possible during planting. Melons need as much heat as possible. In very cold climates such as the Olympic Peninsula they must be grown in a hoophouse or greenhouse.

Seeding Depth: ½ to 1 inch.
Seeding for Transplant: Late April to mid-June. Transplant anytime mid-May to early July.
Direct Seeding: Mid-May through June. Once the soil has warmed.
Plant spacing: 12-24 inches in row, with 3-5 feet between rows.
Soil/Fertility: Moderate fertility is required for healthy plants as is a well-drained soil. Work the soil at least one foot deep and add generous amounts of compost.
Water: Water sparingly at the seedling stage. After planting in the garden, irrigate thoroughly twice weekly, letting soil dry out a bit in between waterings.
Harvest: Any time during fruit set. Fruits are more tender and seeds are smaller when harvested young, but fruits are edible even when they are quite large.
Pests: Mostly insect-free.
Disease: Seedlings are prone to damping off due to cool and overly moist soil. Mature plants can succumb to fungal diseases, powdery mildew is quite common in this area. Provide good drainage and airflow around plants and be cautious not to overwater.
Winter Harvest: Not suitable, harvest fruits before first frosts.

Winter Squash and Pumpkin (*Cucurbita pepo, maxima and moschata*)

General Comments: Pumpkins, acorn and delicata squash are *pepo* types and are the most assured to ripen in a cool location. Buttercups, hubbard and kabocha types are *maxima* and usually require more heat and a longer growing period. Butternut squash are *moschata* types and require the longest and hottest climate to fully ripen. Winter squash come in both bushing and vining varieties and this choice will impact your final spacing. They like warm soil, so there

is no benefit to starting them too early in the season. Early plantings will benefit from the protection of row cover or a cloche. If growing from transplants it is important to minimize plant stress: try not to let plants become root bound in their pots and disturb the roots as little as possible when planting.

Seeding Depth: ½ to 1 inch.

Seeding for Transplant: Late April to mid-May. Cucurbits are prone to damping off in the seedling stage, make sure the soil is warm and irrigate only enough to ensure germination.

Direct Seeding: Early May through late June. Soil must be kept warm during germination.

Plant Spacing: 24-48 inches in row with 3-5 feet between rows.

Soil/Fertility: Needs moderate to high fertility. A well-drained soil is also important for healthy plants. Work the soil deeply and add generous amounts of compost.

Water: Water sparingly at the seedling stage. After planting in the garden, irrigate thoroughly once or twice weekly, letting the soil dry out a bit in between waterings.

Harvest: Leave fruit on the plant until the stem becomes dry and corky or just before the first hard frost, whichever comes first. To properly cure winter squash leave in a warm, dry location for a couple of weeks before storing at cooler (though not cold) temperatures. Attics and greenhouses are great places to cure winter squash. The best place for long term storage is a dry, dark place that is a bit cooler than room temperature, such as a closet.

Pests: Mostly insect-free.

Disease: Seedlings are prone to damping off due to cool and overly moist soil. Mature plants can succumb to fungal diseases. Powdery mildew is quite common in our area. Provide good drainage and airflow around the plants and be cautious not to overwater.

Winter Harvest: Not suitable, harvest fruits before first hard freeze.

Fabaceae Family

Snap pea, Snow pea, Shelling pea (*Pisum sativum*)

General Comments: Peas are generally the first seed to be sown in the garden in late winter/early spring. There are three main types of peas and they all have similar growing requirements. Varieties under 3 feet tall do not require trellising, though harvest is easier if there is some type of support. For tall varieties use fencing, chicken wire or other type of trellising for the plants to grow up. Peas do best when planted in the early season. Later plantings can be attempted if you have a particularly cool or shady garden. Peas may also be sown in dense plantings for their tendrils and cut when very young for fresh or cooking greens.

Seeding Depth: ¾ to 1 inch.

Seeding for Transplant: Late February through March.

Direct Seeding: March through April. Peas can be planted as soon as the soil can be worked, however, there is not much advantage to planting before March.

Avoid planting into waterlogged soil as this may cause the seed to rot. Pre-treat seed with legume inoculant for maximum nitrogen fixation and highest yields. Late season peas can be grown from mid-August sowings, though they are usually not as tasty as spring peas and often succumb to powdery mildew.

Plant Spacing: Up to 15 seeds per foot on both sides of pea fence or support.

Soil/Fertility: Needs moderate fertility with plenty of available phosphorus and calcium. Avoid planting into overly acidic soil. Many gardeners amend soil with lime and a light dusting of wood ashes before planting.

Water: Weekly deep irrigation is necessary for the sweetest and most tender peas. Avoid over-irrigating as this can lead to soil-borne fungal disease.

Harvest: Shelling peas, or English peas, are picked when the full pea can be felt in the pod. The pod is not eaten as it is stringy. Snap peas may be picked any time, though they are sweetest when the peas have just filled out their pod and formed a bulge. The pod is edible and sweet. Snow peas have an edible pod and are usually picked just as the peas begin to form in the pod. All peas should be harvested before they become starchy, (the ability to determine this comes with experience) and eaten as soon as possible after harvesting. Make sure to pick all ripe peas when harvesting to keep the plants producing.

Pests: Mostly insect-free.

Disease: Susceptible to many diseases. The most common is powdery mildew which impacts plants later in the season. This can be avoided by starting peas early in the season and choosing powdery mildew-resistant varieties. Pea root rot (*fusarium*) is also fairly common in this area. This causes the plant to begin drying out from the ground towards the top. Good soil drainage and proper crop rotation help with this.

Winter Harvest: Not suitable for winter harvest.

Legume Inoculants

All legumes (peas, beans and fava beans as well as leguminous cover crops) benefit from a coating of legume inoculant. These are strains of bacteria that create a symbiotic relationship with the plant, allowing it to fix nitrogen in the soil and thereby increasing the vigor of the plant. Most garden stores sell a garden combination inoculant which works with both peas and beans. To apply, put seed to be planted in a bowl, mist the seeds with water and then dust with a small amount of the inoculant. Mix to coat by hand. Do this directly before planting.

Pole bean, Bush bean, Shell bean, Dry bean
(*Phaseolus vulgaris*)

General Comments: Beans are a warm season vegetable, fairly easy to grow and provide great rewards in the late summer garden. Bush varieties require no support and usually have a more concentrated fruit-set, making them a good choice for canning or freezing. Pole beans require something to grow up (fence, twine or poles) and usually fruit over a longer period of time. Beans benefit from treatment with legume inoculant. Bush beans may be grown under row cover for added warmth and earlier harvest. Good drainage is essential.

Seeding Depth: ¾ to 1 inch.

Seeding for Transplant: May through June.

Direct Seeding: Mid-May through July, once the soil has warmed to 55 degrees. Planting beans into cool soil may cause the seed to rot and the plant to be less vigorous. There is no need to rush. Succession sowings may be planted every two weeks through July for a continued harvest.

Plant Spacing: 4 to 6 seeds per foot on all sides of growing support.

Soil/Fertility: Needs low to moderate fertility. Available calcium and phosphorus will grow the strongest plants.

Water: Regular deep irrigation is best, do not overwater.

Harvest: Harvest any time beans have formed. The best fresh-eating beans are picked when young and tender and the bean has yet to fill in the pod. Shell beans are left to mature on the plants until the bean seed is visibly plump through its pod. Dry beans are left to mature on the plant until the pod is fully dried out.

Pests: Mostly insect-free.

Disease: Susceptible to some fungal disease or molds. If this is a problem, plant at a wider spacing to increase airflow around the plants. Soil fusarium can impact beans. To avoid this, practice good crop rotation with at least 3 years between all legumes.

Winter Harvest: Not suitable for winter harvest.

Fava bean (*Vicia faba*)

General Comments: Also known as broad beans, fava beans are the only cool season shell bean around. The pods are not edible, but the tender tendrils are great fresh or steamed. October plantings usually overwinter nicely and mature much earlier than spring plantings. Fava beans also make a great fall-sown winter cover crop. Treat fava beans with legume inoculant before planting. Fava beans do not require any trellising or support.

Seeding Depth: 1 inch.

Seeding for Transplant: Not recommended.

Direct Seeding: February to mid-June and October to early November. Fava seed is more rot-resistant than pea seed.

Plant Spacing: 3 inches in row with rows at least 12 inches apart.

Soil/Fertility: Needs low to moderate fertility. More fertile soil will produce healthier and more productive plants.

Water: Though somewhat tolerant of irregular irrigation, the best beans are grown with weekly deep irrigation during the dry season.

Harvest: When the beans are plump in the pod. Shell before eating. Young tendrils may be harvested at any time, though this may impact overall plant development.

Pests: Aphids are fairly common. They may be sprayed as needed with insecticidal soap to control.

Disease: Fava beans are susceptible to viral disease spread by aphids that can cause the leaves to turn black. Control aphids as needed.

Winter Harvest: The pods are not suitable for winter harvest, though the tendrils are.

Laminaceae Family

Basil (*Ocimum basilicum*)

General Comments: Basil is a tender, warm season annual herb that can be grown in our cool climate with a bit of care. There are many varieties of basil and all have the same growing requirements. In general, wait until it really starts to feel like summer before planting out. Any temperatures below 50 degrees may damage the leaves. Give basil the sunniest, warmest and most protected place in the garden. It may be grown under hoops with plastic covering, under row cover, in cold frames or vented cloches. As basil wants to quickly go to seed, it is important to pinch it back as it grows (see Harvest section below for details on this technique). Basil does well in pots.

Seeding Depth: 1/8 inch.

Seeding for Transplant: Mid-April (if in greenhouse or cold frame)

through June.
Direct Seeding: Late May through July.
Plant spacing: 6-18 inches
apart in all directions.
Soil/Fertility: Needs
moderate fertility and a well-
balanced soil with very good
drainage. Too much
nitrogen can weaken the
flavor of the basil and attract
aphids.
Water: Somewhat finicky
about water requirements.
Water deeply as needed to
keep plant healthy but do
not overwater. For the most

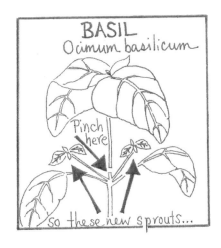

flavorful basil, keep on the dry side. Avoid watering plants late in
the day as wet leaves and cool temperatures at night may cause
damage to the leaves.
Harvest: When the plant is a few inches tall, pinch off the stem
beneath the largest set of
leaves (the terminal bud) at
the top of the plant. This
encourages bushy growth. As
the plant grows through the
season, continue pinching off
the top leaves on each branch
as they get large or begin to
produce flower buds. This
encourages bushy growth and
discourages flower formation.
Harvest the entire plant and
process before the first frost.
Do not store harvested basil in

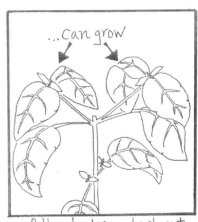

the refrigerator. Place stems in water at room temperature or use
pinched leaves as soon as possible.
Pests: Aphids, control with insecticidal soap as needed. Slugs love

basil, use traps as needed.

Disease: Fungal disease is fairly common. Provide plants with plenty of airflow and a dry growing environment.

Winter Harvest: Very tender, not suitable for winter harvest.

Poaceae Family

Corn (*Zea mays*)

General Comments: Corn is a much loved staple crop native to the Americas. The sweet corn that we are used to eating likes warm summers, which can be hard to come by in our region. There are, however, some extra-early varieties that will mature in our cool summers and germinate in cool soils. Always choose extra-early maturing types known for their cool-soil seedling emergence. As corn is pollinated by wind, for complete pollination plant corn in blocks of 4 rows and not in a single straight row.

Seeding Depth: ¾ to 1 inch.

Seeding for Transplant: The transplant method is recommended for cool locations. Start indoors or in a greenhouse from late April through May. Plan to transplant after all threat of cold weather has passed.

Direct Seeding: Late May to mid-June. Direct seeded corn will greatly benefit from protection with row cover to increase soil temperature during germination.

Plant Spacing: 8-18 inches apart in all directions.

Harvest: Harvest any time after the silks begin to dry back and turn brown. For dry corn, protect with bird netting and keep corn on plant until completely dry.

Soil/Fertility: Needs moderate to high fertility. Well-composted soil with good drainage is best. Will benefit from side-dressing mid-season.

Water: Consistent (at least weekly) deep irrigation.

Pests: Mostly insect-free.

Disease: Damping off is fairly common during germination in cool soils. Plant when soil temperatures have warmed and avoid overwatering.

Winter Harvest: Not suitable for winter harvest.

Solanaceae Family   The Nightshades

Tomato (*Solanum lycopersicum*), Tomatillo and Ground Cherry (*Physallis spp.*)

General Comments: Growing an excellent tomato in this climate is one of the greatest challenges a Maritime Northwest gardener may face. If tomatoes are being grown outdoors, *always* select varieties that are listed as "early maturing." Even if tomatoes are being grown in a greenhouse or hoophouse, choose varieties that mature in less than 80 days for best production. Talk to other gardeners in your micro-climate to find out which varieties perform well for them. Choose determinate or indeterminate varieties to suit your system. Tomatillos and ground cherries are generally grown like tomatoes though they are easier to grow and require less attention. Unless tomatoes are being grown in a greenhouse, it is best to wait until the soil has warmed and most cold weather has passed before setting them into the garden, usually the middle to end of May.

Seeding Depth: ¼ inch.

Seeding for Transplant: Early March through April. Plan seeding so plants are ready to transplant by mid to late May. Cover or protect in some way for the first month.

Direct Seeding: Not recommended.

Plant Spacing: 12 to 24 inches in row with rows spaced at least 3 feet apart.

Soil/Fertility: Needs light to moderate fertility. Tomatoes appreciate a well-composted soil. Avoid high-nitrogen fertilizers as too much nitrogen can cause the plants to grow lush with an excess of leaves and less fruit. Available calcium and phosphorus are essential for good fruit development. Some growers like to add bone meal and rock phosphate to the soil when transplanting.

Water: Consistent, deep irrigation is important in the early stages of growth and fruit development. When fruit begins ripening, water can be cut back a bit. Too much water during ripening can lead to splitting. Tomatoes generally prefer to be watered with drip irrigation. If not using drip irrigation, water gently to avoid splashing water onto the lower leaves by using a gentle stream of water. Wet leaves, especially at nighttime, can lead to disease.

Harvest: Tomatoes are edible at any stage, though best when they have developed color. Depending on the variety, a tomato is mature when it turns deep red, orange, pink, yellow or green-striped.

Pests: Generally insect-free. Flea beetles may eat the leaves of young plants but this does not usually impact fruit development.

Disease: Tomatoes are prone to fungal disease in our climate. The most common is late blight, which can cause lesions on the leaves and stems of the plant. Symptoms of other fungal diseases are leaf spots and dying, burned looking leaves. Few varieties have complete resistance to fungal disease and some amount of disease is normal. (Try not to worry too much!) If the disease becomes worrisome, prune off impacted parts of the plant and destroy by burning (or at the least remove from your garden). Botrytis is another common fungal disease and looks like grey fuzz growing on the stem of the plants and on the stems/tops of the fruits. Remove all infected parts of the plant. All fungal diseases are best avoided by providing plenty of airflow around the plants. If possible, pick and destroy any impacted fruit immediately and remove from the garden. Practice crop rotation to avoid build-up of fungal disease.

Winter Harvest: Not suited for winter harvest, though it is possible to prolong the harvest to the end of November. Before the first hard frost, pull entire tomato plant with roots attached. Bring inside to a moderately warm room and hang from the roots so that the plant is upside down. Some of the remaining fruits will mature.

Determinate and Indeterminate Tomato Plants

There are two basic types of growing habits for tomatoes and it is important to know the difference.

Determinate tomatoes are bush types that may be grown without support (though some varieties do better when properly staked to allow more airflow). They are well-suited to growing in containers or smaller spaces and are best for gardeners who want to be less involved in the process. Determinate tomatoes generally have a more concentrated fruit-set. Pruning is not necessary. Grow tomatillo and ground cherries similarly to a determinate tomato.

Indeterminate tomatoes are often referred to as climbing or vining tomatoes. They continue to grow and produce fruit until the first killing frost. The vines need to be supported by staking, caging or trellising. Pruning is also necessary for indeterminate plants. See below for detailed instructions on how to prune a tomato plant.

How to Prune an Indeterminate Tomato Plant:

The goal of tomato pruning is two-fold. The first is to eliminate some of the potential branch and leaf growth in order to give the plant increased airflow and reduced disease pressure. The second goal is to focus the energy of the plant on just a couple of main branches (often called leaders) so that the plant will put energy into maturing fruit on those branches instead of growing a multitude of new branches, leaves and fruit (which may or may not have time to mature).

⅄ Tomatoes send out branches at the base of each leaf where it meets the stem. Starting at 12 inches up the main stem select two hardy and vigorous branches from the plant. One of these will be the natural main stem, the other will be a side branch. These will be the "leaders" and they will continue to grow during the season. (Figure 1) Prune off any other branches that may exist. (Depending on how old the plant is there may be many or there may be none.)

Figure 1

⅄ Now look at the two leaders. Where each leaf meets the stem of the leader, there is a new branch forming. This happens on every stem at the base of every leaf as the plant grows! These new branches are called suckers. Suckers will vary in size from super tiny to a few inches (or longer if not pinched). Locate a sucker. Using fingers and nails pinch it as close to the base as possible. If it is too big to pinch use clean garden shears. (Figure 2)

Figure 2

⅄ Prune or pinch off any other suckers on each of your two leaders. This process needs to be repeated weekly throughout the season.

(Picture them sucking the power from your ripening tomatoes for motivation to keep up on suckering.)

ʌ Now you have two pruned leaders or branches that need to be trained to grow onto some sort of support. The support needs to be strong enough to hold the branches as they grow and become laden with potentially heavy fruit. There are many options: fencing, tall wooden stakes or t-posts and twine, or tall tomato cages.

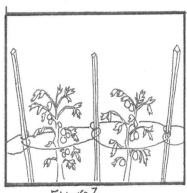

Figure 3

(Figure 3) Tomato cages are sold at garden stores, do not use the short ones for indeterminate varieties. Be creative! The idea is to use whatever materials you can find and fit well into your system and your budget. If using a stake system it is generally a good idea to secure the branches to the support with twine as they grow. Many professional growers gently wrap the tomato onto a piece of heavy twine that is hanging from a secure spot at least 6 feet above the tomato plant. (Figure 4)

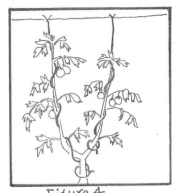

Figure 4

Growing Heat-Loving Crops in a Cool Climate
Tomatoes, Peppers, Eggplants

These plants of the Solanaceae family are tropical plants; they need extra heat and full sun. Always plant varieties known to mature in your specific area. Some varieties do well when grown in pots on a sunny deck next to a building which can provide protection from wind and can radiate heat at night. For planting outside in the ground, full southern exposure is mandatory. Be creative and try to provide a microclimate that is protected in some way (especially from cool wind). Warm soil and warm air will grow the best tropical plants. Fabric row cover can be effective. Low tunnels made from hoops covered with clear plastic can work provided there is some ventilation. The commercially available "Wall O' Water" works well for heating up the soil and protecting young plants. Mini greenhouses are a good investment if you are committed to growing heat-loving crops.

Hot pepper, Sweet pepper (*Capsicum annum*), Eggplant (*Solanum melongena*)

General Comments: Peppers and eggplants require the warmest spot in the garden. In all but the warmest microclimates, some form of protection is necessary to ripen these crops (row cover, slitted plastic, hoophouse, etc.) Choose the earliest ripening varieties even if growing in a greenhouse. A bit of wind or shaking of the plants will help with early pollination and fruit set.
Seeding Depth: ¼ inch.
Seeding for Transplant: March to early April, transplant after all cold weather has passed and protect from cold wind.
Direct Seeding: Not recommended.
Plant Spacing: 12 to 24 inches in all directions.

Soil/Fertility: Good drainage is important as is abundant phosphorus and available calcium. Avoid excess nitrogen as this will result in an increase of leaves and a decrease of fruit.

Water: Consistent moisture is necessary. Water deeply twice a week or as needed. Water may be cut back as fruits begin to ripen. Drip irrigation is helpful for disease control.

Harvest: Harvest when fruit is ripe. Peppers can be harvested when green or yellow, though most sweeten in taste as they mature to red or orange. Eggplants are ready to harvest when the skin turns shiny.

Pests: Flea beetles can be a problem in the early season, though they usually do not impact the plants too much. If this becomes a serious problem, insecticidal soap, neem oil or pyrethrin based sprays may be used as directed.

Disease: Bacterial leaf spot and blights as well as fungal disease. To discourage, use drip irrigation.

Winter Harvest: Harvest all fruit before first hard frost.

Potato (*Solanum tuberosum*)

General Comments: Potatoes are one of the most enjoyable vegetables to grow and harvest. They are relatively easy to produce and may be grown in small spaces. Potatoes are planted from cuttings of other potatoes. To prevent disease it is recommended to use certified seed potatoes. Before planting, let your seed potatoes rest at room temperature for a couple of weeks to initiate sprout formation. A couple of days before planting, cut pieces of potato that are about the size of a small hen's egg, being sure that each piece has at least a couple of sprouts. Let these cuts heal (dry) a bit before planting.

Seeding Depth: Dig a shallow trench and place seed pieces in, cover with 3 inches of soil.

Planting Dates: Early March to early June.

Plant Spacing: 12 inches apart in row with rows at least 3 feet apart.

Hilling: As the potatoes grow, use a hoe to cover a half to two thirds of the plant with a mound of soil. This is not an exact science, just pile some dirt up there. This is called hilling and is an important step in growing potatoes because they grow upward into the soil. Without hilling, yields will be lower and potatoes near the soil surface will turn green from exposure to light. Hill potatoes two or three times during the first 8 weeks of growth.

Soil/Fertility: Potatoes can grow in almost any soil, though a fertile soil will be the most productive. Apply compost in the fall to the area where potatoes will be planted in the spring.

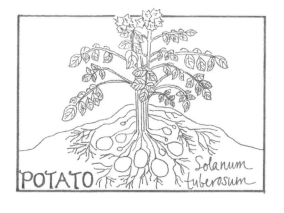

Water: Potatoes can be grown without irrigation, though weekly irrigation will likely encourage healthier, more productive and scab-free potatoes. Stop watering as the plants begin to die back.

Harvest: Any time after the plants begin to flower. At the early flowering stage the potatoes will be small and very tender. For full-sized tubers wait until the plants have begun to die back. To fully cure potatoes for long term storage, leave them in the ground for a couple of weeks after the plant has died back.

Pests: Mostly insect-free. Flea beetle can chew tiny holes in the leaves but do not usually impact growth. Wireworms can be a problem in cool seasons in first-year gardens where the ground has recently been sod.

Disease: Healthy soils full of micro-organisms create the healthiest

potato plants. Some fungal diseases such as blight occur in this
area. A crop rotation of 5 years between all solanaceae family plants
is important. Potato scab is a disease that causes raised scabs on the
skin of the tubers. Scab is controlled by avoiding the use of fresh
manure or unfinished compost on potato beds directly before
planting and by maintaining consistent soil moisture during the
growing season.

Winter Harvest: Potatoes are best harvested before the soil begins
to freeze. Store in a cold, dark place.

Perennials

Asparagaceae Family

Asparagus (*Asparagus officinalis*)

General Comments: A slow-
growing perennial that can last
up to 15 years in the garden. It
may be grown from seed,
however, for quicker
establishment it is grown from
crowns. Even when grown
from crowns, asparagus takes 3
years before it produces any
harvestable shoots. Plant in a
permanent location that
receives full sun and has good
drainage.

From Crowns: Best to purchase
disease-free crowns from a reputable company. Plant in early spring.

From Seed for Transplanting: Start seeds in greenhouse in early

February. Plant seeds ¾ inch deep. Seeds require consistent temperatures of 65 degrees or warmer. Transplant out in early June and treat the same as crowns.

Planting: Start by digging a 6 inch deep trench. Place crowns or seedlings in the trench with the roots laying flat and the crown of the plant pointed upwards. Cover crown with 1-2 inches of soil. Gradually fill in trench as the spears grow the first year. Keep well-weeded during the growing season. Mulch with alder wood chips, sawdust or weed-free straw to keep weeds in check.

Soil/Fertility: Needs moderate to high fertility with plenty of organic matter. Plant crowns into well-drained and well- composted soil with a near neutral (7.0) pH. Add lime if necessary. Top-dress annually with compost.

Water: Water as needed to keep the plants healthy during the dry season, be cautious not to overwater.

Harvest: Do not harvest for the first two seasons, just let it grow. On the third season full harvest may begin. Harvest all shoots for the first 4-5 weeks of production each season. Then allow the remaining stems to mature as this helps to feed the roots.

Pests: Mostly insect-free.

Disease: Rust and fusarium are both potential problems in our area. Choose disease-resistant varieties.

Winter Harvest: Not suitable for winter harvest.

Polygonaceae Family

Rhubarb (*Rheum rhabarbarum*)

General Comments: An easy-to-grow perennial. Grown for its sour tasting, tender stems which can be used like fruit. Leaves contain toxins, eat only the stems. Can be grown from seed or from crowns. Divide plant crown every 8 years to keep vigorous.

From Crowns: Crowns may be purchased from gardening companies or obtained as a division from a rhubarb-growing neighbor or friend in the early spring. Plant crowns in early spring.

From Seed for Transplanting: Sow seeds ½ inch deep in late winter or early spring. Transplant out in 8-10 weeks. Rhubarb grown from seed should not be harvested until the third year in order to give the crown time to develop.

Planting: Choose a permanent, sunny and well-drained location. Give the plant 4 feet in all directions. Place plant in ground so the crown is just at soil level.

Soil/Fertility: Needs low to moderate fertility. Rhubarb is very adaptable. For the most productive plants provide plenty of fertility in the form of compost at planting and top-dress annually with compost. Mulching with straw or alder wood chips helps to retain moisture and reduce weeds.

Water: Water deeply as needed to keep the plants healthy during the dry season. Be careful not to overwater. Mulching helps to retain water.

Harvest: Spring to early summer. (Do not harvest until the plant is well established). When stems have reached a good size pull off at the base of plant. Cut leaves off when harvesting and leave at base of plant as a mulch, do not eat them! Never harvest more than half of the stems in any one season. Stems can become tough and stringy by mid-summer, at that point let plant go to flower.

Pests: Usually insect-free.

Disease: Usually disease-free.

Winter Harvest: Not suitable for winter harvest.

Rosaceae Family

Strawberry (*Fragaria* × *ananassa*)

General Comments: With a little attention garden strawberries are easy to grow and extremely rewarding. A well-cared for crop will be productive for 3 to 4 years before it needs to be replaced with fresh plants. In our region there are two types of strawberries that do well, June-bearing and ever-bearing.

*June-bearing types produce a single, large crop of fruit when the day's light is the longest, during the month of June.

*Ever-bearing, or day neutral, types produce smaller quantities of fruits throughout the growing season as long as temperatures are above freezing.

Growing from Crowns: Most commercial varieties of strawberries are grown from propagated crowns purchased from a nursery. They are available as potted plants or as bare root crowns. It is best to purchase disease-free crowns from a reputable company. Plant in early spring as soon as the soil can be worked. Strawberries may also be grown from runners from a mother plant. Just snip off the runner and plant the new crown.

Starting Seed for Transplanting: Some varieties of strawberries may be grown from seed. The seed is very small so be careful not to plant too deeply.

Planting: Dig a hole large enough to spread the roots into and fill in the soil around the plant, being careful not to fully bury the crown of the plant. Space plants at 12 inches apart in all directions. Planting strawberries into holes cut in black plastic or weed fabric can help control weeds and increase soil temperature. Strawberries do well in containers if not allowed to overcrowd each other.

Growing: Strawberries make runners during the growing season. We recommend pinching these off and letting the mother plant have space to grow. The runners may be replanted, though they will not be as productive as the mother. Letting runners grow unchecked can lead to overcrowding and less productivity.

Soil/Fertility: Needs well-drained moderately fertile soil with plenty of organic matter. Adding bone meal at the time of planting can help with fruit production. Top-dress annually with compost.

Water: Water as needed to keep the plants healthy during the dry season, though be cautious not to overwater. Drip irrigation is best for disease prevention.

Harvest: Pick fruits when red and ripe. Pick off and remove overly ripe and moldy berries.

Pests: Mostly insect-free, though slugs and birds can be a problem.
Disease: Fungal disease can impact strawberries. Select varieties known to do well in your specific area.

Perennial Culinary Herbs

General comments: Perennial herbs have an important place in the kitchen garden. Once established they are easy to care for and should live for many years in the garden with minimal work.
Seeding for Transplanting: Seed in fall or late winter as many perennial herbs need to experience a bit of cold before germinating. Many herb seeds are tiny, be cautious not to plant them too deeply or wash them away with heavy irrigation water. Follow instructions on seed packet closely.
Transplanting: Mid-March through August.
Direct seeding: Not recommended. Seed is often very small and can take very long to germinate.

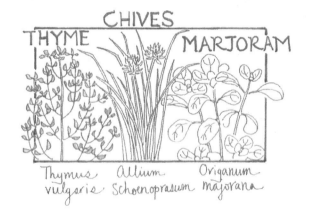

Plant spacing: 12-18 inches apart in all directions (more for large varieties of Rosemary). They can all do well grown in a pot or other container.
Soil/Fertility: Only moderate fertility is needed for perennial herbs. Compost and mulch annually.
Water: Good drainage is essential for all perennials. Give an

occasional, deep watering, avoid overwatering.

Harvest: Harvest sparingly the first year to allow the plant to fully establish a good root system. After that harvest by clipping off sprigs as needed.

Pests: Mostly insect-free.

Disease: Mostly disease-free. Clip off any diseased, dying or dead branches throughout the year.

Growing in Containers: Most herbs do well when grown in containers or pots as long as they have good drainage. It may be necessary to divide the plant after a year or two so it does not become root bound. Be certain to add a bit of compost each year.

Chives (*Allium schoenoprasum*): An easy-to-grow perennial that will provide the first taste of onion in early spring. Chives are usually one of the first herbs to put on significant new growth. Makes wonderful edible flowers mid-season. Will grow under a wide variety of conditions.

Sorrel (*Rumex acetosa*): The northwest "lemon" leaf, great for many culinary uses. This plant does best in rich, moist soil, but will survive almost anywhere. Sorrel is a vigorous self-seeder, clip off the flower stalks to prevent it from taking over the garden.

Mint (*Mentha spp.*): Mint is very easy to grow, though most mints from seed are not that strong in flavor. The best mints are those taken from cuttings of a high quality mother plant. Mint is a vigorous spreader and will take over the garden if not maintained. We recommend either putting it in an out-of-the way area that is suitable for becoming a permanent mint zone or growing it in pots. If grown in a pot it is necessary to divide the plant each spring and give it some new soil. Mint can handle more water than many other perennial herbs. Harvest all of the leaves and dry them for use in the winter before the first hard frost.

The Mediterranean Herbs: All are fairly easy to grow provided they are given a suitable soil and a sunny location. Good drainage is key to longevity of these herbs. Never plant them in an area known to have standing water in the winter. If growing in a container, mix in soil and sand, compost, perlite or tiny gravel to help with drainage. An addition of agricultural lime or dolomitic lime help to maintain a neutral to alkaline soil, which all of these herbs like. For the healthiest plants top-dress with compost and lime annually.

Oregano *(Origanum vulgare)*: Finding a strongly flavored strain will be the hardest thing about growing this plant. Best grown from root cuttings of a known mother plant. If purchasing a plant from a nursery, test the leaves to make sure they have a suitable flavor, in general, no two plants will be the same.

Culinary Sage *(Salvia Officinalis)*: A great plant for its culinary leaves and beautiful flowers. Sage plants usually lose their vigor over time and need to be replaced after about 3-5 years.

Thyme *(Thymus spp.)*: There are many varieties of thyme. English thyme and German Winter thyme are favorites for culinary use. Both produce leaves high in essential oils. German Winter thyme seems to put on more leaf matter just before winter, making it the preferred variety for winter harvesting.

French Tarragon *(Artemesia dracunculus sativa)*: Much more flavorful than Russian tarragon, though it does not produce viable seed so may only be grown from cuttings. French tarragon does well in our area and usually makes it through the winter. The main factor to consider when growing it is to provide a very well-drained soil all through the year. For this reason it will do better in a pot if your garden soil is wet in the winter.

Rosemary *(Rosmarinus officinalis)*: Rosemary can be grown from seed or from cuttings. It will take much longer to reach maturity if started from seed. It likes a very well-drained, almost rocky soil with lots of lime, lots of sun and protection from cold winds. Drainage is important for overwintering a rosemary plant. Rosemary will survive most winters just fine, however in an especially cold year it can freeze to death. To avoid this, either choose a variety that is known to be cold hardy or grow it in a pot that can be brought indoors for protection.

Marjoram (*Origanum majorana*): Marjoram is an easy-to-grow and essential culinary herb. It is considered a tender perennial, though usually grown as an annual in our region. Prefers a sunny spot protected from the wind if possible, though it is quite versatile. Keep cut back to encourage new growth and discourage flowering.

Winter Gardening

One of the greatest joys of gardening near the Salish Sea is the opportunity for winter vegetable harvest. Success will depend upon proper timing. In general, by late autumn it is too late to plant a vegetable garden for harvest that winter. The winter vegetable garden, if it is to be thriving and bountiful, must be planted during the summer months. By mid-autumn the plants must be fully established and grown mostly to full size. The plants put on little to no growth during the winter, during that time the garden is simply a place to hold them so that the gardener may enjoy the fruits of their labor all season long.

Plant growth is regulated by a few different factors. Soil, soil fertility, soil temperature, air temperature and number of daylight hours are the most influential. By late October, when the night temperatures are often near freezing and the days are significantly shorter (and cooler), most plant growth has stopped. The period of time between the Autumnal Equinox and late October is the twilight of plant growth. Knowing that little growth will occur past this time, we plan to have our late autumn and winter garden fully established with the plants close to the desired harvest size by early October.

Planning this requires a little math and a calendar. Let's say, for example, that we want to harvest fresh carrots from the garden throughout the winter. Nothing is more satisfying than a fresh carrot in January that has been sweetened by the frosts. According to the seed packet, a nantes-type carrot may take 70 days (from seedling emergence) to mature. Remember that 70 days is probably just an average and represents the days to maturity when planted in the early spring for summer harvest. When planted in mid-summer for late autumn maturation, it will take longer because the temperature will be steadily decreasing as will the number of daylight hours. To compensate for this, add an extra 10-14 days on to the original 70. Remember also, that the 70 day count begins from the time the seedling emerges (8-12 days, average 10, from planting the seed). So, with all of that in mind, (70+10+10), we need approximately 90 days from the time we plant the carrot seed for it to be full-sized for continuous winter harvest. We want our carrot to reach full size by mid-October when plant growth stops. So we note October 15 as our desired harvest date (or storage in the field), and work backwards from there. October 15 minus 90 days, or three months, brings us to July 15 for our winter carrot sowing date!

The same method may be used for any vegetable we plan to harvest throughout the winter.

Let's use kale as another example, which needs 65 days to reach maturity. While it is true that kale is a hardy crop, it still does not grow much in the winter. We want our kale plant to have what is called a "full frame" by mid-October, so that it will have plenty of leaves on it for a good winter supply. Kale is most often grown from transplants. The 65 days to maturity listed on the seed packet is counted from the day it is transplanted into the garden. 65 days plus 10 days (added for late season slow growth) means that we must transplant the kale plants 75 days before October 15th. The seeds, therefore, must be started the first week of July in order to be ready for transplant by August 1st. Of course, kale may be eaten at any stage, so if we do not get it planted by then we will just have smaller plants going into the winter and that is fine too.

Slower-growing crops such as leeks, Brussels sprouts and parsnips usually take more than 100 days to reach maturity. That means they may need to be started in the spring for winter harvest!

Vegetables that mature more quickly such as Asian turnips, arugula or radishes can be direct seeded into the garden as late as early September.

Winter Hardiness Chart

Light Freeze	Medium Freeze	Hard Freeze
Broccoli	Chard	Leeks
Onions	Baby mustard greens	Carrots
Escarole	Beets	Kale
Some lettuce varieties	Spinach	Rutabaga
Radish	Celery Root	Brussels sprouts
Celery	Arugula	Parsnips
Full sized mustard greens	Green onions	Parsley
Cauliflower	Radicchio	Collard Greens
Peas	Kohlrabi	Purple sprouting broccoli
Pac Choi	Turnips	Overwintering cauliflower
Napa Cabbage	Short to mid-season cabbages	Storage cabbages

Depending on the specific microclimate, some of these vegetables may need a little extra attention to make it through the winter and still be edible. Most of the root vegetables will benefit from mulching or top dressing with a few inches of straw before the year's first really hard freeze. Generally the part of the root that is beneath the soil will be fine, but the part that is at and above the soil line can be damaged by prolonged freezes and the continued freeze/thaw cycle. Mulching the tops provides insulation by retaining some of the earth's natural heat around those vegetable tops. Polyester row cover also can provide a few degrees of frost protection for slightly more tender leafy greens such as chard, escarole and radicchio.

The final treat of the winter garden is that in the spring, many of the surviving plants will begin to grow again. Certain plants may even be planted later in the autumn in order to keep them at a small, immature size through the winter. This provides a measure of protection from hard freezes. In the late winter and early spring the increase in both temperature and daylight hours will induce the plants to put on a lot of delicious, new growth. Some varieties of cauliflower and sprouting broccoli have been bred specifically for this purpose.

For more specific information on sowing dates for the winter garden, please see the information provided under each specific vegetable.

Disease in the Garden

An experienced gardener knows that some plant disease in the garden is fairly common and is usually not cause for alarm. A good approach to plant disease management is to start off by knowing how the plants you grow appear under normal, healthy circumstances. When a plant shows signs of potential disease, you will know that something is wrong. Some of this understanding can only come with experience.

Generally, if you notice a sick looking plant in the vegetable garden it is best just to observe it for a few days - up to a week. Ask yourself: "Could this plant problem be caused by something in the plant's immediate environment?" For example: improper nutrition, too much or too little water, pests, chemicals, wind burn or other stress causing factors. If, after close observation, you are certain that the plant issue is not caused by an environmental condition, the chances are high that you have some variety of plant disease.

Garden diseases can be broken down into 3 main categories: fungal, bacterial and viral. Correctly diagnosing the specific disease can be difficult and complicated. Many symptoms of disease are similar across categories making certain identification difficult. If you have a strong interest in properly identifying plant disease there are numerous helpful websites and books on the topic, please see the resources section in the last chapter.

Oftentimes a plant can grow right through a disease issue and be just fine. At other times a disease can wipe out an entire portion of the garden. If the disease appears to be progressing rapidly and is completely killing plants and/or spreading to other plants, you may need to remove the afflicted plant or plants to prevent further spread of disease. In some cases it is possible to isolate just the infected portion of the plant and remove that part. If only a single leaf on your kale plant looks odd, clip only the impacted leaf or stem. It is best to burn or bury any diseased plant material. Avoid putting diseased plant material in the compost pile as this can spread disease throughout the garden.

A few basic measures can go a long way towards preventing disease from taking hold of your garden. Always provide good airflow around the plants. Be cautious to not overcrowd your garden. Full sunlight throughout the day helps keep leaves dry and plants growing strong. Proper watering is essential in the prevention of disease. Keep soil moisture in the moderate zone, not too wet and too dry. Overly wet soils can lead to build-up of soil borne disease and a soil that is too dry can weaken a plant to the point of being more susceptible to disease. Avoid watering plants late in the day as this increases the likelihood of the leaves being wet through the night, which can lead to the proliferation of both bacteria and fungi on leaf surfaces. Early morning watering is usually the best. It is also important to make certain the plant has the available nutrients it needs as nutrient deficiency can also lead to disease. The final and perhaps most important factor in disease prevention is soil health. A strong plant with a healthy root system in a soil teaming with microscopic life will be much less susceptible.

Most of the plant diseases that impact vegetable gardens near the Salish Sea are fungal. Below are some of the most common.

Club Root is a soil-borne fungus that impacts all plants in the Brassicaceae family (cabbage, broccoli, kale, etc).
Symptoms: Infected plants may appear stunted and may wilt during the hot weather. The roots become swollen and gnarled, impacting the plant's ability to move water and nutrient to the above ground portion.
Prevention: It proliferates in wet, acidic (low pH) soils, so always work your soil deeply and apply agricultural lime before planting. Allow at least a 4 year rotation between growing brassica family crops in the same part of the garden. Reducing the number of brassica crops that are grown is the easiest way to prevent club root. Once a garden is infected with club root it is very difficult to get rid

of as the fungus can live on brassica weeds such as wild mustard and shepherds purse. The only course of action is to destroy impacted plants, stop planting brassica family crops for a few years and raise the soil pH to above 7.2 by adding lime as the fungus cannot live in in alkaline soils.

White Rot of garlic and onions is a fairly common soil-borne fungus in our region as it favors the cool, damp soils common here.
Symptoms: A fairly rapid yellowing of leaves late in the growth cycle, die-back of plant roots and often death of the plant. An infected plant pulls out of the ground easily and will show evidence of white fungal mycelium at the base of the bulbs.
Prevention: White rot does not disperse by spores, but by small black pinhead sized sclerotia which can remain active in the soil for up to 15 years. Once a garden becomes infected with this fungus it is necessary to stop planting any allium family plants for at least 10 years. If symptoms are noticed during the growing season, stop watering immediately and destroy impacted plants. For prevention, always plant garlic seed stock and onion transplants from a disease-free source and be careful not to use any garden tools that have been used in infected soil.

Powdery Mildew is a fungus that impacts vegetables in the cucurbit family (summer squash, cucumbers, winter squash and pumpkins) as well as some leafy greens such as chard.
Symptoms: A white, powdery film forms first on older leaves and then spreads throughout the plant. This leads to a slow decline in health and eventually to a premature death.
Prevention: Choose powdery mildew resistant varieties and maintain consistent soil moisture. Plants grown in overly dry soils are more susceptible. As it is a fairly common disease, try planting succession sowings of cucumber and summer squash to ensure a continued supply throughout the season. Most winter squash and pumpkins will mature fruit even with some amount of the disease. Homemade soapy garlic sprays and baking soda sprays have shown to be somewhat helpful in prevention as well if used diligently on a

weekly basis.

Rust is a fungus associated with garlic, leeks, onions and other alliums, (as well as roses) and is favored by cool, moist climates.
Symptoms: Orange-rust colored, slightly raised spots on the leaf tissue. Rust usually does not kill a plant, though it can slow growth and decrease the general health of the plant.
Prevention: Grow strong plants and practice crop rotation. Weak, water or nutrient-stressed plants are more susceptible. Rust may be effectively controlled by spraying with organically approved fungicides such as copper or sulfur.

Blight is a fungus spread from the soil to the leaves of plants that can impact both tomatoes and to a lesser degree, potatoes.
Symptoms: There are two strains: early and late blight, which both show up on the leaves initially as small spots and progress into large brownish areas. Late blight can progress onto the stems and fruits, with both developing lesions infected with white fungal growth.
Prevention: Use a trellis system to keep the leaves off of the ground, prune off excess foliage, give the plants plenty of air flow and use drip irrigation for all tomatoes. The bottom leaves of the tomato plant are most likely to show disease first, so those can be pruned off as needed. Practice good crop rotation, with at least 5 years between tomatoes, peppers and potatoes grown in the same soil. Dispose of any infected plant material by burning or taking to the dump. Using beneficial bacteria sprays such as compost tea or commercially available Serenade (*Bacillus subtilis*) can be helpful in preventing blight growth if used regularly.

Insects in the Garden

Insects are a wonderful and essential part of every garden. They pollinate some fruit-bearing plants, mix nutrients into the soil and feed on other unwanted insects in the garden. The pest insects in our gardens are harmful only in the sense that they are beating us to the harvest. There are very few insects that will actually do irreparable damage to vegetable plants. While most insect damage is superficial, some infestations can make for an unappealing harvest, or kill or stunt a plant before it can mature. In addition, a plant that is being eaten by insects experiences some amount of stress, making it more susceptible to disease.

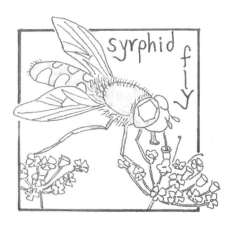

The first step in avoiding insect troubles is to grow healthy stress-free plants by providing them with good soil and proper irrigation. Insects will always choose to feed on weak plants over healthy ones. Secondly, plan and plant for diversity. Include as many different kinds of vegetables, herbs and flowers in your garden as possible. A wide range of flowering plants that bloom throughout the entire growing season will attract and feed a variety of beneficial insects (syrphid flies, parasitoid wasps, lady beetles to name a few) and add to the general flourish of the garden. In a diverse garden most pest problems will work themselves out over time.

Try to include these easy-to-grow flowering plants in the garden: angelica, dill, cilantro (coriander), phacelia, nasturtium, alyssum, calendula, sunflower and borage.

The Most Common Garden Pests
& How to Deal with Them

Aphids are tiny (but visible to the naked eye) gray, green or black insects that feed off the sap of tender vegetables. Aphids usually do not kill the plant. As an effective preventative measure, plant beneficial, insect-attracting flowers in the garden, phacelia in particular.
How to respond? 1. Spray aphids off of the plant with high pressure water. 2. Spray aphids with soapy water or insecticidal soap. 3. If all else has failed (as is often the case with infestations on Brussels sprouts), spray aphids with Neem oil or an organic pyrethrum based spray (be certain to follow the manufacturer's instructions carefully).
Spray only in the early morning before the bees have started to fly.

Cabbage Looper (moth) and Cabbage Worm (butterfly)
larvae love to chew holes into beautiful heads of cabbage and leave droppings behind. They are usually only a problem on heading plants, such as cabbage, Napa cabbage and pac choi, though they will munch the leaves of other brassica family plants. As an effective preventative measure, plant beneficial insect-attracting flowers in the garden, phacelia in particular. Also, cover plants with polyester row cover from the time the plants are in seedling stage until they mature.
How to respond? Hand-pick caterpillars and remove them from the garden.

Brassica Root Maggot is the larvae of a fly that lays its eggs at the base of brassica family plants. The maggots feed on the stem or root of the plant near the soil line, often killing new seedlings or causing lasting damage that can make the vegetable unpleasant to eat, as in the case of edible root brassicas such as turnips or rutabaga. As an effective preventative measure, cover the plants with row cover from the time the plants are seedlings until they

70

mature. Make sure the edges of the row cover are fully buried with soil to keep the fly out. This is generally the only technique that works well.

How to respond? Once you have an infestation, there is not much you can do other than to salvage what you can of your crop. Root crops will be the most affected, but damaged parts can be trimmed off before eating. If they have reached maturity, the heading brassicas (such as cabbage and broccoli), may be stunted but they are still fine to eat.

Carrot Rust Fly deposits its eggs at the base of plants in the Apiaceae family (carrots, parsnips, etc). The ensuing larvae (maggots) feed on the roots of the plant. They usually do not kill the plant but can make it unappealing to eat. Early season plantings are less impacted by rust fly than are summer plantings. Carrots, parsnips and celery root are all impacted by this pest, though celery root to a much lesser degree. As an effective preventative measure, cover the plants with polyester row cover from the time they are seeded until harvest. Make sure to bury all edges of the row cover with soil to keep the fly out. This is generally the only technique that works well.

How to respond? Once there is an infestation there is not much you can do. Trim off affected areas of the plant before eating.

Flea Beetle is a very tiny, black or brown beetle that jumps when disturbed. It feeds on the leaves of many vegetable crops, creating many small holes. Young seedlings that become infested may be killed or stunted, though most plants can outgrow the damage. They are most active once temperatures have warmed up a bit. The most commonly damaged plants in our region are arugula, Asian greens, eggplants and peppers. As an effective preventative measure, cover with polyester row cover from the time of seeding until harvest.

How to respond? There is not much you can do if the flea beetle has found your patch. However, the tiny holes they leave in the leaves of your crops do not affect the quality or taste of your harvest.

Slugs and Snails are not technically insects though they *are* significant and common pests in Salish gardens. Slugs in particular can level a patch of tender seedlings in a single night, leaving behind a trail of slimy mucus as evidence. They like moist, dark places to hide and make babies. To make your garden unattractive to them, keep the surrounding area clean, dry and well trimmed/mowed. **How to respond?** 1. Pick the slugs out of the garden by hand and move them far away, maybe even to slug heaven. 2. Try making a homemade beer slug trap by burying a container full of beer up to the soil level. Empty trap and renew the beer each day.

Wireworms are the larvae of the Click Beetle. They are slender creatures that look like very small, brown, gold or cream-colored worms that live in the soil. Wireworms feed on the roots of plants. In the garden they go for onion seedlings and root crops, burrowing in and feasting. They are usually only a problem in soil that has recently been turned from grass to garden.
How to respond? Avoid planting into cool soil. Wireworms do not like warm soil and will move deeper as the soil warms, leaving vegetable crops unharmed. If wireworms have been a problem in previous years, before planting, work the garden soil as deeply as possible. This disturbs their habitat and they will leave after a few years of deep cultivation. If wireworms have found their way to a crop, spraying the beneficial nematode *Steinernema carpocarse* directly on the soil is moderately effective at controlling wireworm. It is available through mail order companies.

Floating Row Cover

Floating row cover, often called by one of its commercial names, Remay, is a thin, white polyester, fabric that is available in different sizes and weights. It is great both for pest protection and for creating warm micro-climates around garden plants. The down-side of row cover is that using it adds to the already staggering amount of waste plastics in the world. Unfortunately it does not last much longer than a few years before it is torn to shreds, thus it often ends up in the landfill or floating in the Pacific Gyre. Row cover may be laid directly on top of the plants or suspended above the plants by wire, plastic or metal hoops with the ends pushed into the ground.

Row Cover for Pest Protection
Row cover is very effective at excluding pests from crops if used properly. It is important to completely cover the desired vegetables with the row cover from the time they are planted in the garden. Make sure the piece of fabric that is being used is large enough to provide room for the growing crop and has no holes in it. Also make sure *all* edges of the row cover are completely buried in the soil so tiny insects cannot find their way underneath. The most effective way to do this is to shovel a bit of garden soil on the edge of the fabric all the way around. Use enough soil to keep the wind from blowing the row cover off.

Row Cover for Increased Heat and Frost Protection
Row cover may be used to create a micro-climate around garden plants. It works sort of like a greenhouse by trapping some of the sun's heat during the day, retaining some of the earth's heat at night and blocking some of the wind. Using row cover helps early planted vegetables to mature faster and warm season vegetables, such as tomatoes, to ripen more quickly. By increasing soil and air temperatures around the plant, row cover also protects plants from light frost, providing up to 4 degrees of extra warmth. When using row cover on plants that require insects for pollination, make sure to remove it once the flowers begin to form.

Crop Rotation

Crop rotation refers to the practice of rotating plantings of crop families within the available garden space on a schedule that spans a number of years at a time. This prevents members of the same family from being grown in the same area of the garden before it is wise to do so. Proper crop rotation is essential in helping the soil remain healthy and balanced, as some crops take certain nutrients from the soil and others give back nutrients to the soil. Crop rotation also helps avoid the buildup of soil-borne diseases and insect pests associated with certain crops.

For example, beets are susceptible to a fungus in the soil that causes scabs on the skin. If we were to plant beets in the same spot each year, over time the quantities of that fungus would multiply to a point that the beets would be overtaken. If, however, we plant beets one year, then peas the next, then cucumbers on the third year and onions on the fourth year, the beet scab fungus would be deprived of its major host, the beet, and thus diminish in quantity. On the fifth year, it would be safe to plant beets in that spot once again.

There is another piece to add to the rotation puzzle. Think of the four major groups of plant parts as: leaf, root, flower, fruit. We do not want to grow crops from the same group two seasons in a row. For instance, we would not follow a season of beets (grown for their root) with a season of potatoes (though technically a tuber, also grown as a root crop). They are from different plant families, but both being root crops, they may be susceptible to some of the same soil-borne diseases and insect pests. Therefore, instead of growing potatoes on year two, we might plant a flower crop such as a leguminous cover crop or a bed of annual flowers. Most importantly, we would plant anything other than a root crop or a member of the *Amaranthaceae* (beet) family.

The rotation a gardener chooses will depend upon how many crop families are grown in the garden. It is highly recommended to have at least 4 crop families and at least a 4 year rotation between those families. Members of the *Brassicaceae* (brassica), *Amaryllidaceae* (onion, garlic) and *Solanaceae* (tomato, potato) families are the most susceptible to soil-borne diseases and thus should be given the longest rotations in the garden. If space allows, it is good to have as long of a rotation as possible. However, it is important to remember that in a home garden, a picture-perfect crop rotation may not always be possible. Above all, be observant and enjoy the process!

For effective crop rotation it is incredibly helpful to create annual maps of the garden. Do not expect that you will retain this information in your memory from one year to the next. Accurate labeling of what crops were planted where and when is essential. Keep these maps in a folder that is easy to reference at planting time the following season.

A sample 5 year rotation: 5 garden beds and 5 crop families

	Bed 1	Bed 2	Bed 3	Bed 4	Bed 5
Year 1	Kale and cabbage	Carrots and beets	Legumes or cover crop	Cucumber and pumpkin	Onions and garlic
Year 2	Carrots and beets	Legumes or cover crop	Cucumber and pumpkin	Onions and garlic	Kale and cabbage
Year 3	Legumes or cover crop	Cucumber and pumpkin	Onions and garlic	Kale and cabbage	Carrots and beets
Year 4	Cucumber and pumpkin	Onions and garlic	Kale and cabbage	Carrots and beets	Legumes or cover crop
Year 5	Onions and garlic	Kale and cabbage	Carrots and beets	Legumes or cover crop	Cucumber and pumpkin
Year 6	Kale and cabbage	Carrots and beets	Legumes or cover crop	Cucumber and pumpkin	Onions and garlic

Cover Cropping

A cover crop is a crop that is grown for the purpose of improving soil fertility, preventing soil erosion, outcompeting weeds and giving the soil a break from the hard work of growing annual vegetables. Cover crops scavenge nutrients from the soil and then release them when they are decomposing in the soil. Cover crops are planted very densely as to cover all of the soil in the areas being planted and turned into the soil all at one time. They are usually broken down into two categories: winter cover crops and spring/summer cover crops.

Winter cover crops are planted in the early fall, allowed to grow slowly through the winter and then mowed and incorporated into the soil just as they begin to flower in the late spring. Winter cover crops include: the nitrogen fixing legumes (peas, vetch and fava beans) and cereal grains (rye and oats), among others. A combination of a cereal grains and legumes mixed at a 50/50 ratio can supply the soil with a generous amount of nitrogen and organic matter to fuel the next round of crops. For the most nitrogen fixing action, be sure to inoculate any legume seed with legume inoculant.

Spring and summer sown cover crops are usually quick-growing plants that can easily be added into a crop rotation. They are mowed and incorporated into the soil just as they begin to flower, before mature seed is formed. The most commonly used in our climate are buckwheat and phacelia. Both buckwheat and phacelia attract numerous beneficial insects to the garden when in flower. Though in the case of buckwheat if it is allowed to flower for too long, the stems grow more fibrous and are more difficult to incorporate into the soil.

Resources

Seed Companies

Seed Dreams, Rare, heirloom Seeds
Port Townsend, WA 98368
www.seeddreams.blogspot.com/
gowantoseed@yahoo.com

Oatsplanter Farm, Open-pollinated, non-GMO, organically grown
and locally adapted seed
PO Box 1751
Port Townsend, WA 98368
360-385-2135
www.oatsplanterfarm.blogspot.com

Uprising Seeds, Organic and heirloom seeds, grown by Northwest
farmers
2208 Iron St.
Bellingham, WA 98225
360-778-3749
www.uprisingorganics.com

Wild Garden Seed, Organic heirloom and open-pollinated seed
adapted to the Pacific Northwest
P.O. Box 1509
Philomath, OR 97370
541-929-4068

Siskiyou Seeds, High quality, organic, biodynamic seed
3220 East Fork Rd.
Williams, OR 97544
541-846-9233
www.sevenseedsfarm.com

Territorial Seeds, Organic and non-organic seeds for Northwest gardeners
PO Box 158
Cottage Grove, OR 97424
1-800-626-0866
www.territorialseed.com

Osborne Seeds, Organic and non-organic seed for farmers, good source for cover crop seed
2428 Old Hwy 99 South Road
Mount Vernon, WA 98273
360-424-SEED (7333)
http://www.osborneseed.com

Irish Eyes Garden Seeds, Regional seed company, great organic garlic and potato seed
Eastern, WA
509- 933-7150
www.irisheyesgardenseeds.com

Johnny's Seeds, High quality seeds and tools for farmers and gardeners
P.O. Box 299
Waterville, Maine 04903
1-877-564-6697
www.johnnyseeds.com

High Mowing Seeds, Organic seeds, open-pollinated and hybrid seeds
76 Quarry Rd.
Wolcott, VT 05680
802-472-6174
www.highmowingseeds.com

Seeds of Change, Organic seed
P.O. Box 4908
Rancho Dominguez, CA 90224

888-762-7333
www.seedsofchange.com

Fedco Seeds, Cooperatively owned seed company, good variety, great catalog
PO Box 1520
Waterville, ME 04903
207-873-7333
www.fedcoseeds.com

Salt Spring Seeds, Heritage and heirloom organic seed
Box 444, Ganges P.O.
Salt Spring Island,
BC, V8K 2W1 Canada
(250) 537.5269
www.saltspringseeds.com

West Coast Seeds, Organic, open-pollinated and heirloom seeds for West Coast BC gardeners
3925 64th Street, RR#1
Delta, British Columbia
Canada, V4K 3N2
1-888-804-8820
www.westcoastseeds.com

Seed Growing

Seed to Seed, by Suzanne Ashworth (Chelsea Green Publishing)
Seed saving and growing techniques for vegetable gardeners.

Breed your own Vegetable Varieties, by Carol Deppe (Little, Brown and Company)
General information on plant genetics and breeding.

Organic Seed Alliance (OSA)
OSA advances the ethical development and stewardship of the genetic resources of agricultural seed through collaborative

education, advisory services, and research programs with organic farmers and other seed professionals.
www.seedalliance.org

Gardening Tools and Supplies

Peaceful Valley Farm and Garden Supply
888- 784-1722
www.groworganic.com

Drip Works
Irrigation supplies with a specialty in drip systems
190 Sanhedrin Circle
Willits, CA 95490
800-522-3747
www.dripworks.com

Arbico Organics
Natural pest control solutions, a great source for live insects and nematodes
10831 N. Mavinee Dr. Ste. 185
Oro Valley, AZ 85737
800-827-2847
www.arbico-organics.com

Gardening

Botany for Gardeners, by Brian Capon (Timber Press)
A clear explanation on how and why plants grow.

The Maritime Northwest Garden Guide by Seattle Tilth Association
A great month-by-month garden guide, useful website with loads of tips.
www.seattletilth.org

Growing Vegetables West of the Cascades by Steve Solomon (Sassquatch Books)
A comprehensive book about growing vegetables in our region.
www.soilandhealth.org

How to Grow More Vegetables by John Jeavons (Ten Speed Press)
A classic book for those interested in bio-intensive gardening techniques.
www.johnjeavons.info/

Herbs for the Pacific Northwest by Moira Carlson (Steller Press Limited)
An informative and easy-to-read and -use guide for those interested in herb growing.

Permaculture: A Designers Manual by Bill Mollison (Tagari Publications)
An all-inclusive textbook-style read covering everything from garden design to soil microbiology.

Weeds of the West, by Tom D. Whitson, et al. (University of Wyoming Agricultural Extension)
An extensive and easy to use guide of over 900 plants with color photos.

Washington State University Extension
Extensive information for NW gardeners.
www.gardening.wsu.edu

Soil and Composting

Teaming with Microbes by Jeff Lownfels and Wayne Lewis (Timber Press)
Explains the soil food web that exists in the garden and how to cultivate it.

Let it Rot, the Gardeners Guide to Composting by Stu Campbell (Storey Books)
An enjoyable, light read and classic on backyard composting.

Rodale Book of Composting, by Deborah Martin and Grace Gershuny (Rodale Press)
A comprehensive look at composting for gardeners and farmers.

The Soul of Soil by Grace Gershuny, Joe Smillie (Chelsea Green Publishing)
A Soil-Building Guide for Gardeners and Farmers.

Disease and Insects

The Organic Gardener's Handbook of Natural Insect and Disease Control by Ellis and Bradley (Rodale Press)
The most useful book we have found for insect and disease identification and treatment.

University of California Davis Integrated Pest Management Program
Very useful website with insect and disease identification and management suggestions.
www.ipm.ucdavis.edu/

Soil Testing

A & L Agricultural Labs
General lab services and soil analysis.
10220 SW Nimbus Ave. Bldg. K-9
Portland, OR 97223
503- 968-9225
www.al-labs-west.com/sections/anservices

Twiss Analytical Labs
Washington based lab services and soil analysis.
26276 Twelve Trees Lane, Suite C

Poulsbo, WA 98370
360-779-5141
www.twisslabs.com

Kinsey Ag Services
Soil analysis based on the Albrecht method of soil fertility, compost analysis and fertility recommendations.
97 County Highway 357
Charleston, Missouri 63834
573-683-3880
www.kinseyag.com

AgriChem Analytical (British Columbia)
Salt Spring Island 250-538-1712
Cowichan Valley 250-466-7661
www.agrichem.ca